D0984514

HOUSING ECONOMICS AND PUBLIC POLICY

STUDIES IN PLANNING

General Editors: Brian Bayliss and Geoffrey Heal

Published

Ian S. Jones: Urban Transport Appraisal
Ray Robinson: Housing Economics and Public Policy

Housing Economics and Public Policy

Ray Robinson

School of Social Sciences
University of Sussex

WITHDRAWN
FROM
UNIVERSITY OF PENNSYLVANIA
LIBRARIES

© Ray Robinson 1979

All rights reserved. No part of this publication
may be reproduced or transmitted, in any form or
by any means, without permission.

First published 1979 by
THE MACMILLAN PRESS LTD
London and Basingstoke
Associated companies in Delhi Dublin
Hong Kong Johannesburg Lagos Melbourne
New York Singapore and Tokyo

Printed in Great Britain by
Unwin Brothers Ltd.
Old Woking
Surrey

British Library Cataloguing in Publication Data

Robinson, Ray
    Housing economics and public policy – (Studies
    in planning).
    1. Housing policy – Great Britain
    I. Title   II. Series
    338.4'7'301540941   HD7333.A3

    ISBN 0–333–17785–1
    ISBN 0–333–21107–3   Pbk.

This book is sold subject to the standard conditions
of the Net Book Agreement.

The paperback edition of this book is sold subject to the
condition that it shall not, by way of trade or otherwise, be
lent, resold, hired out, or otherwise circulated without the
publisher's prior consent, in any form of binding or cover
other than that in which it is published and without a similar
condition including this condition being imposed on the
subsequent purchaser.

FINE ARTS

HD
7333
A3
R62

UNIVERSITY
OF
PENNSYLVANIA
LIBRARIES

Contents

Acknowledgements

My thanks are due to numerous people who have helped me with this work. Peter Holmes, Julian Le Grand and Peter West read various chapters and made many helpful suggestions. Christine Robinson and Mimi O'Reilly typed the manuscript with remarkable speed and precision at a time when the shortage of secretarial resources at Sussex placed them under considerable pressure. My wife, Janice, has given me endless support in terms of both general encouragement and laborious proof-reading. Finally, my children, Martha and Alice, have shown an understanding beyond their years in moderating their playtime noise so that their father could work undisturbed.

The author and publishers wish to thank the Controller of Her Majesty's Stationery Office for permission to include material from H.M.S.O. publications.

Introduction

On hearing that he was to be appointed Minister of Housing in a newly formed Conservative government, a recent holder of that position is alleged to have exclaimed that he was ideally suited for the post, owning, as he did, two lovely houses of his own. Though no doubt apocryphal, this story does illustrate one important fact about housing: its universal consumption provides everyone with some first-hand experience of the subject. Unlike the Minister, however, many people have cause for a rather less sanguine outlook. Problems associated with rising house prices, mortgage payments and Local Authority rents; with the inability to obtain adequate loans for house purchase; with slum housing conditions or life in a modern tower block; with shortages of rented accommodation and homelessness; and numerous other adverse aspects of housing in the 1970s are likely to constitute the predominant milieu for opinions on housing. In short, concern about housing usually stems from dissatisfaction with its provision.

Shortcomings in the provision of housing in turn often result from the failure of successive government policies in this area. Too often these have lacked direction and consistency. Crouch and Wolf have described housing policy as 'a series of historical accretions reflecting different and sometimes contradictory policy intentions and changing fashions [that] have combined to produce a mass of anomalies'.[1] It is perhaps a sad comment on these policies that after nearly sixty years of direct government involvement in housing affairs, the late Anthony Crosland should find it necessary to deliver the following judgement: 'I was astounded to find, on taking over as Secretary of State, how flimsy was the basis on which housing policy was then built. No one had any clear idea how many houses the country needed or where. No one seemed to have compared the help given to owner-occupiers on the one hand and tenants on the other. Perhaps less surprisingly, there was no attempt to see how we could achieve greater equality in the distribution of the housing we have available. I am convinced that we need a firmer foundation than that for housing policy. . . . to get beyond a housing policy of "ad hocery" and crisis management and to find out precisely what needs to be done if we are to get on top of this desperate social problem once and for all.'[2]

Crosland's response was to instigate a thorough review of housing policy in order to establish the facts. And certainly, many of the deficiencies of policy have resulted from a lack of knowledge about the housing situation. But others have been attributable to a lack of understanding of the way in which the housing market functions. Frequently there has been a failure to appreciate the spill-over effects of intervention in particular parts of the market. The neglect of this area by professional economists for many years did nothing to improve this state of affairs. Recently, however, the general growth of urban studies has led to an awakening of interest in the subject of housing on the part of a number of economists,[3] although somewhat ironically, it has often been transport economists who have been among the first to display this interest: a group whose initial professional encounters with housing were as obstacles to road building programmes! Whether this increased participation by economists will lead to any improvement in housing performance remains to be seen,[4] but the work they have carried out to date has already increased our understanding of the way in which the market functions and the role of policy within it. It is, therefore, an apposite time to take stock of the progress made so far. At the time of writing, however, there is no British book which brings together the sometimes disparate work that has been carried out on the economics of housing and policy in recent years. In the early stages of the development of the specialism, Lionel Needleman's book, *The Economics of Housing* (Needleman, 1965), performed this function, but this is now out of print and in any case, much work has appeared since it was written. It is this gap in the literature that this book aims to fill.

It has been written for the reader who has an understanding of the principles of basic micro-economic theory and wishes to see how it can be applied to the subject of housing. An attempt is made throughout to combine selected pieces of theoretical analysis with the results produced by empirical research. Sometimes this means that, because of space limitations, particular pieces of theoretical material cannot always be developed at great length if empirical evidence on the subject under consideration is also to be included. In such cases, the reader is provided with detailed references to literature that develops the relevant points in greater depth. Another point worth mentioning at this stage is that the book is more concerned with general principles than detailed descriptions of individual markets and policies. The advantage of this approach is that it makes it easier to appreciate the general processes at work. Its disadvantage is that much of the complexity of, for example, the way that housing legislation is implemented at the grassroots level is neglected. Once again, however, references are provided for readers who wish to pursue these points beyond the bounds of this book. The final point to note concerning the general approach adopted is the extensive use made of North American material. To some extent this reflects the large amount of work that has been conducted on housing economics in the United States in particular, where urban economics has been established as an area of specialisation for far longer than it has been in Britain. However, US material has not been used indiscriminately: only those parts have been selected which have particular relevance for the British reader because of the methodology employed and/or the results they produce. At the same time some comparative analysis often provides useful insights on particular domestic problems.

The book is divided into three parts. The first provides a perspective for an examination of housing by looking at various concepts and institutions that will be encountered frequently in the body of the book, and by describing some of the salient features of the British housing stock. The second part is concerned with market analysis. Thus Chapter Three describes various models of the housing market, while Chapters Four and Five consider, in more detail, the demand for and supply of housing. Placing a discussion of market models before detailed consideration of the component demand and supply relationships represents a reversal of normal procedures. Usually, the constituent parts of a model are examined before they are incorporated into a full model. (Thus single equations are usually specified before they are brought together as a system of equations.) The reason for the reversal in this instance is that we have not presented a single market model but a variety of models each of which emphasises different facets of the housing market. These are, therefore, discussed in a 'global' fashion before more detailed consideration is given to the conditions of demand and supply which underlie them. Finally, the third part of the book investigates a selected number of policy issues. There is, of course, a vast agenda from which any number of policy issues could have been chosen, but once again space limitations dictate some selectivity. Accordingly, four topics have been chosen that each combine the properties of being viewed as housing 'problems' and being amenable to economic analysis. These are rent control, urban renewal, local authority housing and the distribution of housing subsidies.

PART ONE

Perspectives

CHAPTER ONE

Concepts and Institutions

This book examines the operation of the housing market and the role of government policy within it through the application of microeconomic methods of analysis. Although the theoretical apparatus it employs is perfectly general and can be found in most areas of applied economics, the housing market does have certain special features which condition the way in which the analysis is conducted. Accordingly, some preliminary discussion is devoted to them.

Definitions and Measurement

A problem that anyone concerned with housing matters will encounter at a very early stage involves the definition and measurement of a unit of housing. First, when dealing with a durable commodity such as housing, it is useful to draw a distinction between the *stock* of housing and the *flow* of services it yields per period of time. Among other things this distinction provides the basis for the two measures of value commonly encountered in the housing market. These are *rent*, which is the payment made for a flow of housing services received over a specified period of time,[1] and *price*, which is the capital value associated with a particular unit of the stock. In a perfect market there will, of course, be a direct link between these two measures because the price of a dwelling will be equal to the present discounted value of the future rent payments which it is expected to produce minus its discounted operating costs. (In the case of the private landlord these rent payments will be real, whereas for the owner-occupier they will be only imputed, but the principle is the same in both cases.) This relationship may be expressed as follows:

$$P = \sum_{j=1}^{n} r_j (1 + i)^{-j}, \tag{1.1}$$

where P = price, r_j = net rent in period j, i.e. rent minus operating costs, and i = the discount rate.

Furthermore, if we assume that the rent remains constant from period to period and that the dwelling has an infinite life, then in a perfect market where the rate of return obtainable on investments in housing is the same as the rate obtainable on any other asset of equal risk, liquidity, etc., the relationship between the market price of the dwelling (P'), its rent (r) and the market discount rate (i) may be expressed even more simply as follows:

$$P' = \frac{r}{i} \qquad (1.2)$$

However, as we shall see in subsequent chapters, there are many imperfections in the housing market which prevent the attainment of this neat equilibrium condition.

A second complication associated with the definition and measurement of housing arises because of the *heterogeneity* of the commodity. This tends to present problems when it is necessary to make comparisons between individual dwellings or to aggregate dwellings to obtain a total stock figure. Of course, this problem is by no means unique to housing. The trend towards greater product complexity and differentiation in most economies means that it applies to some extent to most consumer products. But it is probably more pronounced in the case of housing. For example, the following list – which is by no means exhaustive – indicates some of the factors which will distinguish one dwelling from another: total dwelling floorspace; plot size; number, size and composition of rooms; structural design, that is, detached, terraced, number of storeys, etc., and internal layout; age; condition of internal and external repair; heating, lighting and plumbing arrangements; garage facilities and so on. In addition, houses will vary in terms of their neighbourhood environments. Factors such as the layout of the streets, the incidence of green space and trees, the presence (or absence) of vehicles and any associated noise and/or air pollution, and various other manifestations of residential quality will all affect the desirability of otherwise identical dwellings. Finally, the location of a dwelling in relation to workplaces, schools, shopping and recreational facilities will determine its accessibility and thereby affect the form of housing services it provides.

Olsen (1969) has suggested that an index of the total quantity of housing services offered jointly by all these aspects of a dwelling is provided by its price. But other writers have chosen to emphasise the multi-dimensional aspect of housing by viewing each dwelling as a bundle, or vector, of 'attributes' rather than a single homogeneous commodity.[2] For example, a typical dwelling k could be considered to offer X_k housing services per unit of time, where the level of service is some function of the dwelling attributes. That is,

$$X_k = X(A_{1k}, A_{2k}, \ldots, A_{nk}), \qquad (1.3)$$

where A_{1k} = total floorspace of the kth dwelling, A_{2k} = number of rooms in the kth dwelling, etc. When particular attributes are relatively homogeneous and quantitative in form, they can be measured straightforwardly in the appropriate units, for example square metres of floorspace, age in years, distance in miles from the workplace centre. However, some attributes reflect qualitative variations and cannot therefore be measured in this way. In such cases, one commonly-used procedure is to express attribute variations in terms of a simple numerical scale. For instance, the state of internal repair may be given a score in the range 1 to 6, such that, excellent condition (= 1), very good (= 2), good (= 3), average (= 4), poor (= 5), and unfit (= 6). This procedure may simply entail ordinal rankings but subsequent analysis often requires cardinality. This tends to introduce a larger degree of subjectivity and danger of inconsistency than is involved in the case of more easily quantified variables, but it is generally felt to be justifiable given the importance of qualitative features and the need to incorporate them in the analysis in some way.

The relative importance of each attribute in the provision of housing services can be measured by estimating the contribution that each one makes to the overall dwelling price. That is, the overall price is viewed as the sum of the individual attribute quantities multiplied by their implicit prices. Various studies that have done this are discussed in Chapter Three. However, it is probably worth noting at this stage that for this procedure to be valid it is necessary for a uniform set of attribute prices to apply throughout the market, or at least in the particular section of the market under examination. But as we have already suggested, there are likely to be numerous sources of market imperfection in the housing sector which will lead to this requirement being violated. None the less, despite its obvious shortcomings, this may be the best procedure available.

Durability

As well as giving rise to complicated problems of measurement, the durability of the housing stock has at least two other important implications. One of these is that it is rarely possible to speak of a housing market being in long-run equilibrium. This is because at any point in time the supply of housing services will be determined largely by the existing stock of dwellings − a stock which will have been built up over a considerable number of years stretching into the distant past. For example, in Britain nearly one-third of the present stock was built before 1918 (see Chapter Two). Only the small proportion of new housing constructed each year (usually under 2 per cent) will reflect current demand and supply conditions; the remainder will be the cumulative legacy of demand and supply conditions in past years and, as such, much of it will be ill-suited to present requirements because of its size, design, spatial distribution, etc. This has led Turvey to comment that 'each town must be examined separately and historically. The features of London, for example, can be fully understood only by investigating its past; it is as it is because it was as it was'.[3] Turvey does, however, go on to argue that equilibrium analysis can nevertheless contribute towards understanding the operation of the property market. For example, while the stock of housing may be fixed, the allocation of individual dwellings and the pattern of rents remains to be determined. Moreover, as we shall see in later chapters of this book, equilibrium analysis can help to explain these and a variety of similar processes, even though the state of equilibrium may never be achieved.

A second implication of house durability is that it makes possible the separation of ownership and use. This has led to the development of a rental market in housing as well as one based upon owner-occupation. On the supply side, the scope for renting arises directly from product durability: because housing is not used up rapidly through occupation, the same dwelling may continue to be offered for renting over a considerable number of years. (The same principle has, of course, led to the emergence of certain other consumer durable rental markets, for example televisions, cars, etc.) On the demand side, renting has long been an important feature of the housing market because of the high price of the commodity. This has meant that the majority of households have been unable to buy their homes outright, and have therefore have had to have recourse to renting. At present nearly 50 per cent of households still rent their dwellings, either in the public or private sectors (see Chapter Two).

Location

The location of a dwelling was mentioned earlier as one of a number of housing attributes. However, this aspect of housing is of such fundamental importance that it warrants separate attention. In essence, location is of interest because it determines accessibility, that is, the time and money costs that must be borne by a household in travelling from its home to the various destinations that it wishes to visit (workplaces, shopping centres, recreational facilities, etc.). Within any given housing area, there will usually be substantial variations in relative accessibility and these will make otherwise identical houses poor substitutes for each other. As far as the demand for housing at different locations is concerned, most households wish to avoid travel expenditures and are, therefore, usually willing to pay a price directly related to a dwelling's accessibility. However, the supply of sites within a given area will obviously be limited, and so the actual allocation of dwelling sites will be determined via a competitive bidding process between households[4] (see Chapter Three).

In the longer term, however, there will be variations in the supply of dwellings with given locational attributes. Building at higher densities represents one way in which these occur. Also, because access is ultimately a function of the transport system, the construction of a new road or rail link, or technological developments reducing the time and/or cost of travel, will have a similar effect. Moreover, trip destinations may change. For example, new facilities may be located on green field sites or other locations that alter the relative accessibility of existing dwellings. Thus the relative access costs associated with a given location do not remain constant. They change through time and thereby cause shifts in demand for particular dwellings. However, as we saw in the previous section, long-run changes of this sort, together with the durable nature of housing, often constitute a source of disequilibrium – in this case, spatial disequilibrium. Thus, in many cities a part of the housing stock is located in areas where there is greatly reduced demand for it compared with previous years. Similarly, at the national level, population movements can lead to excessive vacancy ratios in some regions while excess demand is concentrated on an inadequate stock elsewhere. The physical immobility of housing will prevent these situations being rectified by the transport of the commodity – as would be the case in many other markets – and so the disequilibrium will persist.

Transactions Costs and Imperfect Information

The costs of moving are expensive in terms of time, money and psychic expenditure. This is particularly true for the owner-occupier who wishes to sell a house in one area and buy another at a distant location, but it also applies to local movers and movement within the rental sector. The costs of search, the legal costs payable to 'exchange' professionals (that is, solicitors, estate agents, surveyors, etc.) and the actual expenses incurred in the removal of house contents all combine to produce substantial transactions costs. An implication of this is that adjustments in housing consumption take place less frequently in response to price and income changes, or as a result of changes in family circumstances, than would otherwise be the case. Thus transactions costs represent a barrier to mobility and can be a source of market distortion.

To appreciate this point, consider the way in which a household may be expected to react to a change in family size and the associated change in house space requirements. For example, suppose that family size falls as children grow up and leave home. This will present the opportunity for reducing housing consumption and using the income so released to buy other goods. Formally, we may say that the household will adopt this course of action and move if:

$$|U(\Delta h)| \quad < \quad |U(\Delta x)|$$

$$< \quad |\frac{U(Ph.\Delta h)}{(Px)}|, \tag{1.4}$$

where $U(\Delta h)$ is the loss in utility resulting from a reduction in housing consumption equal to Δh, and $U(\Delta x) = U(Ph.\Delta h/Px)$ is the increase in utility resulting from the additional consumption of a non-housing good x, the actual increase in consumption being equal to the money released by the reduction in housing expenditure, $Ph.\Delta h$ (where Ph is the price per unit of housing services) divided by Px (the price of the non-housing good). However, as we have stressed, transactions involving housing are not costless, so that equation (1.4) should be modified as follows:

$$|U(\Delta h)| \quad < \quad |U\frac{(Ph.\Delta h - T(h))}{(Px)}|. \tag{1.5}$$

Hence the money available to spend on non-housing goods is reduced by the amount of the transactions costs, $T(h)$. This will tend to diminish the probability of a gain in utility resulting from a change in consumption patterns, will act against a move taking place and, in this case, increase the likelihood of under-occupation.

A further consequence of these heavy transactions costs is a high incidence of consumer ignorance within the housing market. Because the costs of moving are so high, the majority of households do not acquire information through entering the market unless some extraneous factor makes it necessary. And unless a household is actively contemplating a move the incentive to acquire information is low. Even among those households who have decided to move, a large number will make decisions on the basis of highly imperfect information because the known time costs of search are high (despite the growth of an information industry, viz. estate agencies) whereas the benefits – in the form of useful information – likely to be acquired through additional amounts of search are uncertain.

The Capital Market

Average dwelling prices are typically two or three times greater than average earnings and for this reason few households are in a position to buy a dwelling outright from their current earnings and accumulated savings. Accordingly the majority of households require access to loan finance if they are to buy a house. Moreover, the high loan/income ratio means that repayment periods need to be spread over a long period of time if the average borrower is to be able to repay the loan from his current income stream. To meet this requirement a number of specialist institutions have grown up that are prepared to offer private long-term loans of up to thirty-five years. The most important of these are building societies, which specialise in loans for house purchase and have, in recent years, been the source of approximately 80 per cent of institutional lending for this purpose.

Building societies grew up in the eighteenth century as savings clubs which used their funds to finance the construction of housing for their members. Originally, the societies terminated when all their members were housed, but in the nineteenth century the present-day practice of extending membership to shareholders and depositors – who simply required a savings account with interest – was introduced. Today there are nearly 17 million depositors and shareholders with around 400 building societies. One feature that distinguishes the societies from other financial intermediaries is that they borrow short-term and lend long – the reverse of normal practice. Thus while loans are offered for up to thirty-five years, depositors and shareholders are free to withdraw their money within days or weeks. The highly liquid nature of their liabilities (and the illiquidity of their assets) makes the societies highly risk averse.

This risk aversion is particularly noticeable as far as their lending policies are concerned, where they operate a stringent set of rules governing the types of property on which they are willing to lend money, the amounts they are willing to lend and the individuals to whom they will lend. These criteria have been criticised by some writers on the grounds that they reflect excessive caution, or even positive discrimination against certain groups and housing areas (Harloe *et al.*, 1974), rather than the real risks associated with different types of loans. For example, it is argued that building societies discriminate against manual workers because their requirements of prospective borrowers' incomes favour those occupations with stable, incremental scales at the expense of those occupations where the earnings profile is more uneven (although no less in present value terms) and/or includes a substantial overtime payments component. Similarly, the unwillingness of the societies to lend on older properties (sometimes referred to as 'redlining' when whole areas are involved) has been cited as a reason for the accelerated decay of certain inner city districts. In reply to these charges, the societies point out their special position in the money market and their need to avoid any semblance of a threat to public confidence in their financial soundness.

Another important aspect of building societies' behaviour is their preference for non-price methods of loan rationing. Hadjimatheou (1976) has argued that the typical society's objective is the maximisation of mortgage loans subject to a minimum reserve ratio and a 'socially acceptable' mortgage interest rate. The second constraint refers not only to the level of the rate, which needs to be competitive with other institutional rates seeking to attract funds, but also the reluctance of societies to vary their rate too frequently. This reluctance arises for two main reasons. First, in Britain – unlike, for example, the United States – changes in mortgage rates are applied to both new and existing borrowers. Hence an increase in the rate will represent a cost of living rise for over four million borrowers. Political pressures and their own concern with their public image make the societies reluctant to undertake such unpopular measures. Second, the administrative costs of changing the rate and notifying borrowers are substantial. Thus in the period 1970–75, the recommended mortgage rate specified by the Council of the Building Societies Association changed only five times, compared with twenty-four changes in the Bank of England's minimum lending rate over the same period. This means that mortgage funds are usually rationed by non-price measures, such as the loan-to-house value or loan-to-income ratio that the society is willing to offer, and so it is often the availability of credit rather than its cost which determines housing demand.[5]

Government and Housing

No discussion of the UK housing market can proceed very far without recognising the central role played by the government. Its policies at both the national and local level determine to some extent the terms on which all housing is demanded and supplied. In categorising its numerous policies it is possible to divide them into three main groups. First, there are those concerned with the direct provision of housing. In the United Kingdom 30 per cent of the housing stock is owned by Local Authorities. Most of this was built by (or for) the LAs who allocate it to tenants and charge rents according to various administrative criteria. This housing is therefore largely removed from the market sector although, as we shall see in Chapter Eight, it is affected by general market conditions, and in turn has an effect on the remainder of the housing market. The second category of policies covers those which regulate the terms on which housing is supplied by the private sector. Among these, public health standards (which determine the fitness of a dwelling for habitation), land-use planning policies dealing with slum clearance, and rent control legislation, are three areas which we shall be discussing in the third part of this book. Finally, there are central government 'tax-expenditure' policies (such as those offering tax relief on house mortgage interest payments, housing subsidies to LAs, etc.) and monetary policies (which determine the availability and price of credit for house purchase and building) which regulate the tempo and the allocative/distributive functions of the market.

While the impact of government policy has been considerable, the rationale and objectives of this policy, and the means by which these objectives are pursued, have often been confused and ill-defined. As the comments of the late Anthony Crosland and others quoted in the Introduction have indicated, policy has been dominated by short-term palliatives resulting in an accretion of anomalies and inconsistencies. Part Three of this book contains a good deal of evidence to support this dismal view. But hopefully it will also provide some clearer insights into the operation of this market and suggest some policy directions for the future.

CHAPTER TWO

A Short Profile of Housing Conditions

Figure 2.1 shows the stock of dwellings and the number of households in England and Wales at decennial intervals between 1911 and 1971. The figures indicate that until 1961 there were more households than dwellings, but that by 1971 this inequality had been reversed: there were nearly a quarter of a million more dwellings than households. However, these figures should be interpreted with caution. Comparisons between the aggregate number of dwellings and households can be misleading if they are used to establish the extent of housing 'shortages' or 'surpluses'. One reason for this is that the number of households is not independent of the number of dwellings. To some extent household formation rates are constrained by dwelling availability. Another reason is that such figures do not reveal the extent of regional and local shortages. If these are pronounced, a national surplus may be of limited use given the well-known spatial immobility of many households. And, in fact, the number of vacant dwellings in 1971 was over twice as large as the excess of total

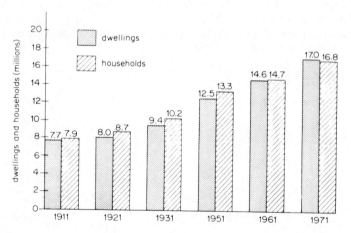

Figure 2.1 Households and the stock of dwellings, England and Wales, 1911–71

Source: *Housing Policy* (H.M.S.O., 1977), *Technical Volume*, part 1, table 1.5, p. 15.

dwellings over households, with the result that over 800 thousand households were sharing dwellings.

By 1971 the stock of dwellings had reached 17 million, an increase of 2.4 million dwellings (that is, about 16 per cent) over the number of ten years earlier. Over the whole period 1911–71, the annual increase in the size of the stock averaged between 1 and 2 per cent. This relatively slow rate of increase is directly attributable to the durability of housing which results in a stock that is the cumulative total of many years' production. Thus Figure 2.2 shows that nearly one-third of the housing stock standing at December 1975 was built before 1918. We have already argued that this legacy of housing from the past will have implications for the equilibrium of the housing market and, as we shall see below, this is reflected to some extent in the condition of much of the older housing.

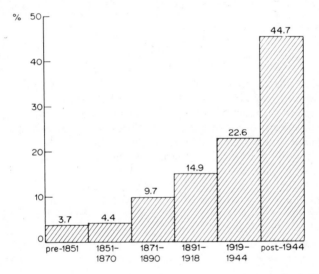

Figure 2.2   Age distribution of the housing stock (December 1975)

Source: *Housing and Construction Statistics.*

Figure 2.3 shows that although the annual percentage increases in the size of the housing stock may be small, these nevertheless represent substantial fluctuations in the rate of *new* housebuilding. For example, in the ten-year period 1965–75 there was a drop in the total number of annual completions of over 144 thousand houses (that is, 35 per cent) between the peak year of 1968 and the trough year

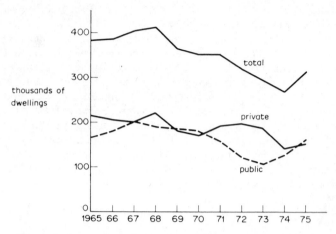

Figure 2.3   New housebuilding: annual completions, 1965–75

Source: *Housing and Construction Statistics.*

of 1974. The breakdown of total completions between public and private housebuilding shows that substantial variations in activity occurred in both sectors, although it was rather more pronounced in the public sector where there was a peak-to-trough fall of 47 per cent compared with a fall of 37 per cent in the private sector. (As far as the housebuilding industry is concerned, it should be noted that much public sector housing is built by contractors drawn from the private sector.) Chapter Five discusses the effect of these fluctuations on the structure and performance of the construction industry.

The changing composition of housing tenure in the post-war period is illustrated in Figure 2.4. Several marked trends are immediately apparent. Most noticeably, there has been a substantial and continuing decline in the relative size of the private rented sector. Between 1947 and 1975 this contracted from a position where it accounted for approximately 60 per cent of households to one where it represented 16 per cent of dwellings. (The incidence of multiple occupancy in the private rented sector is likely to lead to a larger proportion of households being found there than the proportion of dwellings. Thus the drop from 60 per cent of households to 16 per cent of dwellings is likely to overstate slightly the extent of the decline in this sector. But even after allowing for some possible discrepancies from this source, the decline remains dramatically large.) Moreover, as we shall see in Chapter Six, it has not only been a decline in relative size. At the same time, there have been corresponding increases in the

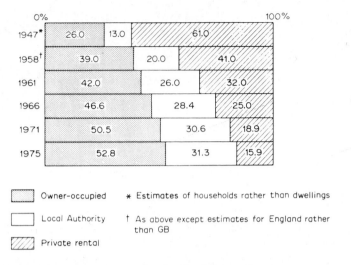

Figure 2.4 Housing tenure: its distribution in selected post-war years

Sources: *Housing and Construction Statistics*, and Donnison (1967) table 10, p. 186

size of both the owner-occupied and the Local Authority housing sectors. The owner-occupied sector is now the single largest tenure category representing nearly 53 per cent of dwellings, having doubled its relative share since 1947. Similarly, the LA sector has experienced rapid growth, increasing its share from 13 to 30 per cent of dwellings. Many of these compositional changes can be attributed to the various forms of government policy that we shall be discussing in the third part of this book.

The relationship between tenure, age and the condition of the housing stock is indicated in Table 2.1. This shows the clear association between age and unfitness:[1] in all tenure categories the proportion of unfit housing is significantly greater among dwellings built before 1919 than it is among those built in the post-1919 period. But age is not the only correlate of unfitness. The proportion of pre-1919, privately rented housing that is unfit (22.5 per cent) is substantially higher than the proportions found in the other two tenure categories. The preliminary results of the 1976 English House Condition Survey confirm this tendency by showing that although the proportion of unfit housing has fallen between 1971 and 1976 (from over 7 per cent of the total housing stock to less than 5 per cent), the proportion of unfit housing in the privately rented sector (nearly 15

TABLE 2.1
Housing tenure, age and condition

Age/Fitness	Tenure class							
	Owner-occupied		Local Authority		Other*		All tenures†	
Built before 1919	000s	%	000s	%	000s	%	000s	%
Unfit	345	3.8	50	1.0	634	22.5	1 202	7.0
Not unfit	2 742	30.3	126	2.7	1 335	47.3	4 364	25.5
Built 1919–71								
Unfit	10	0.1	8	0.2	11	0.4	42	0.3
Not unfit	5 975	65.8	4 599	96.1	841	29.8	11 492	67.2
TOTAL	9 072	100.0	4 783	100.0	2 821	100.0	17 100	100.0

*Mainly private rented.
†Includes a small number of vacant and closed tenancies not listed.
Source: *Housing Condition Survey of England and Wales* (Department of the Environment, 1971).

per cent) remains far above the proportions found elsewhere. (Unfortunately the preliminary results of the 1976 survey do not include a breakdown by age of dwelling and so they cannot be used for the first part of the above analysis.)

The concentration of substandard housing in the private rented sector is confirmed by information on the numbers of dwellings lacking basic amenities given in Table 2.2. This shows that over a quarter of private rented dwellings lack one or more basic amenities compared with only about 5 per cent of owner-occupied and LA housing. Some of the reasons for the concentration of poor quality housing in this sector are considered in Chapter Six.

The final point worth noting in connection with substandard housing is that while there is no evidence to suggest that it is heavily concentrated in particular regions or conurbations, there is evidence of spatial concentration at a more local level. Table 2.3 shows the proportion of total households that lack selected basic amenities or who live in overcrowded conditions that are found in the 'worst' census enumeration districts. (The average census enumeration district contains approximately 150 households. The 'worst' districts have been selected for each quality 'indicator' by taking the 5 or 15 per cent that contain the highest number of households lacking the basic amenity in question or living in overcrowded conditions.) Clearly, the 'worst' EDs contain a disproportionately high share of poor housing. However, its concentration is probably even higher than these figures suggest. In the same study from which the results given in Table 2.3

TABLE 2.2
Housing tenure and the lack of basic amenities

Amenity Lacked	Tenure							
	Owner-occupied		Local Authority		Other*		All tenures	
	000s	%	000s	%	000s	%	000s	%
1. W.C. inside dwelling	360	3.8	157	3.3	437	19.1	1 083	6.3
2. Fixed bath in bathroom	247	2.6	45	0.9	382	16.7	800	4.7
3. Wash basin	293	3.1	139	2.9	427	18.7	991	5.8
4. Sink	6	0.1	1	–	11	0.5	43	0.3
5. Hot and cold water at three points	358	3.8	161	3.4	499	21.8	1 173	6.9
6. One or more of the above	473	5.0	269	5.6	585	25.6	1 493	8.7

*Mainly private rented.
Source: *English House Condition Survey, 1976* (Department of the Environment, Press Notice, June 1977).

TABLE 2.3
*The spatial concentration of poor quality housing in Great Britain,
1971*

Households	Proportion in the 'worst' 5% of EDs	Proportion in the 'worst' 15% of EDs
1. Share or lack hot water	23	53
2. Lack fixed bath	30	64
3. Lack inside WC	28	61
4. More than 1.5 persons per room	33	61
5. Share dwellings	51	83

Source: Holtermann (1975).

have been taken, Holtermann (1975) examines the incidence of poor housing within the major conurbations. She finds that in the 'core' area of Greater London, for example, 94 per cent of households in the worst 5 per cent of EDs lack exclusive use of the five basic amenities listed in Table 2.2, whereas only 47 per cent of total households in the 'core' area lack these amenities. Moreover, the same pattern is found on Merseyside, Tyneside, in Manchester and the other main conurbation areas. Some of the factors leading to the growth of these concentrations of low-quality housing are discussed in Chapter Seven.

PART TWO

Market Analysis

CHAPTER THREE

Models of the Housing Market

Economic studies of the housing market have taken many forms. There have been those which concentrate on macro-behaviour through the formulation and econometric estimation of aggregate demand and supply relationships. Whitehead (1974) in her econometric study of the UK housing market provides a good example of this type of approach. Other studies have been more concerned with the operation of particular local markets. Through these, the micro aspects of housing market behaviour, especially its spatial dimension, tend to receive special attention. Ball and Kirwan's study of the Bristol market (Ball and Kirwan, 1975) is representative of this approach. Still others have taken specific aspects of market behaviour as their focus of attention and examined them from either a purely theoretical, or from a theoretical and empirical point of view. Those which have looked at residential location (for example, Alonso, 1964; Muth, 1969; and Evans, 1973), the filtering process (Grigsby, 1963) and the determination of relative house prices (Wilkinson, 1971), all fall into this category.

The purpose of this chapter is to provide some indication of the theoretical analysis and empirical research that has gone into these various types of studies. Moreover, in so doing, we shall pay particular attention to the way in which the special features of the housing market discussed in Chapter One have been incorporated into different models. At this stage we shall concentrate on the way the market operates within the constraints set by the public sector, leaving analysis of these constraints to later chapters.

Capital Stock Adjustment Models

Housing is an extremely durable commodity and, therefore, in any short-run period of time the supply of housing services will be determined largely by the stock of existing housing: a stock which the age distribution of housing given in Figure 2.1 shows has been built up over a considerable number of years. A corollary of this is that changes in the size of the stock will take place only slowly as even high rates of new construction will represent but a small proportion of the total stock. (In Britain new construction usually represents less than 2 per cent of the stock each year.) This means that the supply of housing services is often slow to adjust to changes in demand conditions, and for this reason an analysis of demand and supply in terms of a disequilibrium capital stock adjustment model is likely to provide a more realistic representation of the market than a conventional single-period equilibrium model.

Figure 3.1 represents such a model diagrammatically: its main features are similar to those appearing in models used by Muth (1960) and Whitehead (1974).

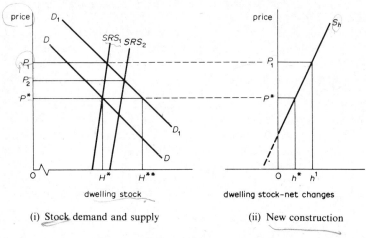

Figure 3.1   Housing demand and supply

In Figure 3.1 (i) *DD* represents the stock demand for housing; that is, the stock that will be demanded (for the flow of services it provides each period) at different price levels, given the population size and structure, their incomes, housing preferences, etc. At this point, no distinction is made between the demand for housing for rental purposes and for owner-occupation. In the same diagram, the schedule SRS_1 indicates the short-run stock supply of housing – a supply that is almost fixed but which may exhibit some elasticity as additions to the available supply, and withdrawals from it, may take place as the price at which houses are traded varies. This could arise, for example, if the speed at which vacated houses are placed on the market varies with price. In such cases a more rapid velocity of turnover would result in a reduction in the vacancy ratio. In the case of the rental market, the elasticity is likely to arise because of the more, or less, intensive use of the potential stock of rental housing associated with different rent levels. But in total these marginal variations will be unimportant in comparison with the overall supply.

The second part of the diagram – Figure 3.1 (ii) – shows the short-run supply schedule for new housing. It is drawn on the assumption that the rate of new construction is a function of current house prices. This involves two major simplifications. First, as we shall see in Chapter Five, it is likely that the behaviour of construction firms is based more upon expectations about future price levels than upon current prices. None the less, existing prices together with prices in the recent past are likely to provide one indicator of future prices and so for the moment we shall retain our initial assumption.[1] Second, there will be a time-lag between the decision to start work and the date of building completion. This means that new building added to the stock will be a function of past price levels. For simplicity, we have assumed a time-lag of a single period so that additions to the stock are a function of the previous period's stock price. Now the net change in the stock between each period will be equal to new construction minus losses which arise through obsolescence and demolitions. If the latter category is technically determined by the age distribution and the size of the stock, then the rate of new construction will be the major variable source of changes in the supply of housing. Let us examine rather more closely the way in which such changes can be expected to take place.

Within the model the interaction of the stock demand and supply conditions determine a short-run market price for housing; this is shown in the conventional way in Figure 3.1 (i) at the point of intersection between DD and SRS_1. Now if the price so established is one at which the rate of new construction is just sufficient to maintain a constant stock through time, we may describe the market as being in long-run equilibrium. Thus in the figure, a long-run equilibrium is achieved at a price of P^* and a stock of OH^*, with new construction equal to $0h^*$. If, however, this equilibrium is disturbed a sequence of changes will be set in motion. For example, suppose there is an increase in the demand for housing, resulting from, say, an increase in mortgage credit availability. This may be depicted by a second demand schedule D_1D_1. This will result in the price of the housing stock being bid up to P_1, which will, in turn, provide an inducement for construction firms to increase their output of new housing to $0h^1$. This will lead to an increase in the stock of housing in the following period: an increase which is depicted by a new supply schedule SRS_2. In consequence, the price of housing will fall to P_2, but as this is still above the long-run equilibrium level, the inducement to expand the stock will remain. Thus a further rightward shift in the SRS schedule will ensue in the following period. This process will continue until a new stock equilibrium, appropriate to the changed demand conditions, is reached at $0H^{**}$.[2]

However, in reality, there are likely to be a number of reasons why a steady convergence towards a new equilibrium will not take place in this well-behaved fashion. One complication is that demand conditions are likely to vary continuously from period to period rather than in the once-and-for-all fashion described in the model.

Thus, instead of observing a steady convergence towards a new equilibrium stock, the equilibrium stock will itself be changing through time. The change in the actual stock in each period will not therefore be a simple lagged response to a single change sometime in the past, but the cumulative result of a series of past changes. This process is illustrated in Figure 3.2 where it is assumed that each discrete change in demand would, *ceteris paribus*, be satisfied by the stock supply change completed after four periods. In addition, we assume that a separate and uniform change in demand occurs in each period so that a series of lagged adjustments will overlap each other. Hence in period 0 there is a change in stock resulting from demand

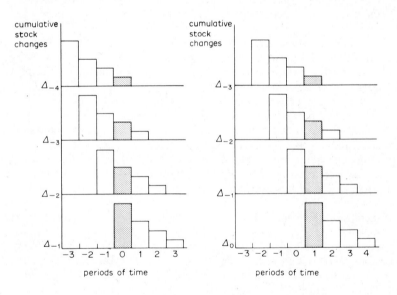

Cumulative, stock change in Period 0   Cumulative stock change in Period 1

where Δ_0 = Stock change resulting from demand change in period   0
Δ_{-1} =   „   „   „   „   „   „   „   „ -1
Δ_{-2} =   „   „   „   „   „   „   „   „ -2
          Etc.

Figure 3.2   Distributed/lagged changes in housing stock

changes in periods −1, −2, −3 and −4; in period 1 the stock adjustments follow changes in demand in periods 0, −1, −2, −3, and so on. Of course, the more frequent the changes in demand, and the longer the distributed lag response to any single change, the more complex the process becomes.

Another complication is that, as Blank and Winnick (1953) pointed out some years ago, changes in demand may not be immediately transmitted to changes in prices but may, in the short run, be absorbed by changes in the vacancy rate. This will conceal the need for stock adjustments and delay responses in the building industry, with the result that when price changes do occur they tend to be violent and cyclical. A likely sequence of events is depicted in Figure 3.3, which is based on a presentation of the Blank and Winnick hypothesis used by Needleman (1965) pp. 153–7.

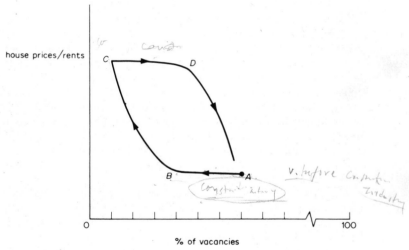

Figure 3.3   Cycles in prices and vacancy rates

The cycle starts at point *A* when prices are low and the percentage of dwellings that are vacant is high. When demand increases the initial response of landlords and sellers accustomed to a depressed market is to continue to trade at unchanged prices. Thus the vacancy rate falls – as more dwellings are demanded – but there is no price incentive encouraging the construction industry to provide more dwellings. This situation persists in the range *A* to *B*. After a time, however, if demand continues to rise, the increased rate of turnover in housing can be expected to induce some upward revision of prices. Once this upward movement is under way it will gather momentum rapidly as sellers/landlords realise that demand is strong and can sustain price increases. During this period prices can be expected to rise sufficiently to initiate new building activity; however, problems of forecasting and time-lags in the construction industry make it extremely likely that supply will overshoot demand. This position will correspond to point *C* in Figure 3.3. With excess supply, prices will stop rising, but price falls will initially be avoided at the expense of an increase in the vacancy rate. Once again, therefore, the price change necessary to induce the building industry to respond is suppressed and, in this case, houses continue to be built at a price where there is no demand for them. This takes place in the range *C* to *D*. At some point however, sellers/landlords will attempt to dispose of their property by cutting prices, and this will initiate a period of rapid price fall until the bottom of the next slump is reached, at point *A* or thereabouts. This slump will persist until demand once again rises sufficiently to reduce vacancies *and* raise prices.

Complications of the type described above are probably sufficiently important to prevent the attainment of a long-run stock equilibrium in the housing market. (See Whitehead and Odling–Smee, 1975.) Nevertheless the concept of an equilibrium or optimal stock is of considerable use in predicting the way the market will behave. For example, we shall see in Chapter Four that it is possible to measure optimum-stock elasticities of demand, even though we cannot measure the optimum stock itself. And as the optimal quantity constitutes the behavioural basis for actual demand, it provides valuable information on the way that demand can be expected to change through time.

The preceding discussion shows how housing stock adjustment models represent a useful device for analysing aggregate market behaviour through time. They can also be used to analyse the dynamic behaviour within particular housing sub-markets when the dwellings and other housing circumstances (tenure categories, location, etc.) are reasonably homogeneous. They are not, however, ideally designed to focus attention on the micro price-determining process. For this purpose, it is necessary to concentrate on the way in which individual buyers and sellers interact through market transactions. This level of analysis becomes particularly important when there is a het-erogeneous housing stock. In such cases it is of interest to examine the way individual houses are allocated and their relative prices determined, and to analyse the links between individual houses or, at a slightly more aggregative level, between different sub-markets.

Ceilings, Floors and Prices

Following Turvey (1957), we shall assume that within a given market both buyers and sellers are well informed about prices and that transactions will take place if they yield gains to both parties – either pecuniary or non-pecuniary. We may start by considering a simple situation in which there is a single dwelling, its owner, and a prospective buyer. The buyer will consider the collection of attributes that the dwelling represents and on the basis of his valuation of these attributes, he will decide upon the maximum price that he would be willing to pay for the dwelling. We may refer to this price as his 'ceiling' price. At the same time the owner will have a minimum price for which he would be willing to sell his house. We shall designate this his 'floor' price. It will, no doubt, depend on whether any extraneous factor, such as a change of job, makes him wish to sell his house, and the price he requires to obtain alternative housing or to realise other expenditure plans. Now if the buyer's ceiling price is above the seller's floor price, we would expect a transaction to take place because it would yield a net benefit to both parties. The exact price at which it takes place will depend upon the respective bargaining strengths of the buyer and seller, although we can be sure that it will be within the limits set by the floor and ceiling. Similarly, if there are two or more prospective buyers for the same dwelling, each of whom has a ceiling price above the seller's floor price, we would expect a transaction to take place. On this occasion we would expect the buyer with the higher ceiling price to obtain the property at a price just above his competitor's ceiling price.

The same general principles also apply in situations where there are multiple buyers and sellers. If the dwelling stock is homogeneous, conventional demand and supply schedules can be used to aggregate individual buyers' and sellers' ceiling and floor prices, and to indicate the number of dwellings that will be sold at the (uniform) market price. If, on the other hand, the housing is heterogeneous, the aggregation necessary for the construction of these demand and supply schedules is not possible. Consequently some alternative formulation is necessary to model the house allocation and price-determination process. A matrix approach of the type presented below provides one possible formulation.

Housing Matrices

For purposes of illustration, the example presented in Figure 3.4 has been confined to a simple situation in which there are just five houses and five prospective buyers, although, as we shall see below, it can be extended to cover situations involving any number of buyers (m) and sellers (n), including those where $m \neq n$. In the example, each house represents a different combination of attributes and the buyers' valuations of each house vary according to their preferences and incomes. The elements in the matrix indicate the ceiling prices which different buyers place on each of the dwellings. For ease of exposition it has been assumed that there is a common preference ordering shared by all five buyers, although the intensities of their preferences vary. The right-hand column shows the floor price set for each dwelling by its seller. Finally, the matrix refers to a single period of time.

House \ Buyer	A	B	C	D	E	Floor prices
1	60	52	45	40	35	50
2	50	46	41	35	34	40
3	45	40	38	34	30	32
4	40	36	32	30	26	25
5	34	32	30	28	25	20

Figure 3.4   Market ceiling prices

From the matrix in Figure 3.4, it can be seen that buyer A has a higher ceiling price than anyone else for all five dwellings. Moreover, as his ceiling price is also always above the seller's floor price, he could succeed in buying any one of them. However, we would predict that he will tend to choose the dwelling that yields him the largest net benefit; that is, the one which maximises the difference between his ceiling price and the actual market price. This condition is likely to be satisfied if he chooses dwelling (1), for the excess of A's ceiling price over that of *B* (£8000) is greater than in the case of any other dwelling. Once *A* has made his choice (and assuming the possibility of buying second homes is precluded), *B* is in a position to buy any one of the remaining four dwellings. However, he too will tend to choose the dwelling which offers the highest net benefit; in his case it is likely to be dwelling (2). And so the allocation procedure continues. In this instance, the matrix has been constructed so that the sequential allocation process results in the set of buyer–house combinations shown on the diagonal. But other outcomes are obviously possible. For example, consider the introduction of another buyer with ceiling prices of 65, 55, 50, 45 and 40 in the place of buyer *E*. Let us call him buyer *F*. Now it is likely that *F* will buy dwelling (1) and each of the other buyers will, in consequence, be shifted to the next dwelling in the matrix row. If, on the other hand, *F*'s ceiling prices were 43, 37, 35, 32 and 30, yet another pattern of allocation and set of prices would result.

So far, the examples selected have been confined to a single period in which each buyer and seller has engaged in a transaction and the market has been cleared, but this will not always be the case. For example, there may be occasions when no buyer has a ceiling price that is equal to or above a seller's floor price, and hence no transaction will take place. Alternatively, there may be more buyers than sellers, or more sellers than buyers; in the former case some buyers would fail to obtain a house, whereas in the latter some dwellings would remain unsold. Circumstances such as these would probably lead to those buyers/sellers who were unable to realise their plans re-entering the market in the following period, although they may well revise their floor/ceiling prices on the basis of their past experiences. To take account of such behaviour through time we could construct a series of time-specific matrices. These would enable us to investigate the linkages between both demand and supply conditions in successive periods. In short, whenever it is of interest to trace through a linked sequence of market events, the matrix method provides a convenient form of analysis.[3]

One writer who uses this method to investigate the way that changes which occur in one part of the market are transmitted to, and affect, other parts is Grigsby (1963). To examine the mechanisms involved, he concentrates on a series of sub-markets (instead of individual dwellings and buyers) which he views as being related to each other through a continuum of links, for example tenure links, location links, house type links. It is these links which express the degree of substitutability between sub-markets and lead to observations of cross-elasticity effects. However, given the complexity of each individual sub-market, and the linkages between them, Grigsby does not think it feasible to construct a single matrix which deals simultaneously with all their interdependencies. Instead, he uses the approach to throw some light on two specific areas where changes in certain sub-markets can be expected to have implications for the whole market: these are the way in which changes in occupancy patterns result from changes in demand, and the way in which changes in property values result from supply changes. Both of these aspects of housing market performance are directly relevant to the 'filtering' process, which is one of the main mechanisms through which linkages manifest themselves.[4]

Filtering

Heilbrun defines filtering as a process 'which takes place when housing occupied by a higher income group is released by them and becomes available at a lower cost to tenants with lower incomes'.[5] This definition follows closely the traditional view formulated originally by Ratcliff (1949), in which the process is seen as involving both a decline in property values and a change in occupancy.[6] The chain is set in motion initially by households in high or middle income brackets who move into newly constructed housing. Lowry (1960) argues that the impetus for these moves will arise because of changes in tastes which take place over time: these, he argues, will make the housing presently occupied by higher income groups appear obsolete in terms of style and technology compared with new housing. Having a preference for modernity they will move to new housing incorporating more up-to-date features and amenities. As the housing they vacate is usually superior in quality to that occupied by households in the next highest income group it will be attractive to them. However, if there is no change in income and/or population (and hence in demand conditions), the price of the vacated property will have to fall somewhat before this group can afford to take up the additional supply. If they do take it up, then the property they vacate will, in turn, become available to the next group in the income distribution. And so, it is argued, the process will continue.

Filtering has for many years been the subject of a policy debate concerning the most efficient way of improving housing standards for low-income groups. One school of thought argues that benefits will be transmitted via the filtering process to all income groups as a result of new housing built for higher income groups. Advocates of this point of view generally favour private market provision of housing as a means of raising overall standards. Their opponents argue that housing will not filter sufficiently far or fast to benefit those at the bottom of the housing chain. Certainly the limited empirical evidence which is available does tend to cast doubt upon the efficiency of filtering. For example, Firestone (1951) in an early Canadian study traced the chain of moves that resulted from the construction of 500 new units. He found that following the initial moves, the number of dwellings vacated in the four successive rounds were 127, 35, 9 and 1. He concluded that 'the filtering process cannot be counted on to provide a significant number of additional dwellings vacated as a result of a large increase in the volume of newly built homes'. Rather more fragmented evidence for the United Kingdom also suggests that filtering has failed to raise the housing standards of lower income groups. For example, during the period of substantial private house building in the 1930s, it failed to have a marked impact because the rate at which newly formed middle-income households grew was greater than the rate of new construction.

More recently, a study of household movement carried out by Jones (1976) suggests that housing chains may exhibit some unexpected features. His results showed that a surprisingly large number of movers within the owner-occupied sector spent less on the house they purchased than they received on the one they sold. In total, 62 per cent of a sample drawn from the Manchester area traded down in this way. However, this pattern of buying was not reflected in a reduction in the quantity of housing space consumed, nor in the provision of amenities and is not, therefore, directly in conflict with those versions of the filtering process which simply maintain that households will attempt to improve their housing conditions. The results are, however, at variance with the more general notion that filtering is associated with the 'trading-up' of housing. Jones offered two possible explanations for this apparent paradox. One is that some households were adjusting their housing expenditures downwards following a decline in income in the recent past. This does, however, suggest an implausibly widespread number of downward adjustments, especially given the well-known barriers to mobility in the housing market. An alternative explanation is that households may accept an initial qualitative decline in housing services so that they can invest any capital gains made on the sale of their previous housing in dwelling improvements of their own choosing. The availability of improvement grants would obviously encourage this process.

Relative House Prices

In earlier sections a good deal has been said about the way in which the forces of demand and supply interact to determine house prices. In this section we shall be concerned with some of the empirical work that has been carried out to try to identify the quantitative importance of different factors in the determination of relative house prices.

Ball (1973) provides a convenient survey of some of the more important empirical studies of relative house price determination that have been carried out in recent years. He shows that although the approaches of individual researchers have varied there have been certain assumptions and methodological procedures that have been common to most studies. Most notably, there has been general acceptance of the view of housing as a collection of attributes. Accordingly, a dwelling price is usually defined as the sum of expenditures on each of its component attributes. These in turn can be expressed as the product of the quantity of each attribute and its price. Hence:

$$P_i = a_1 A_{i1} + a_2 A_{i2} + a_3 A_{i3} + \ldots + a_n A_{in}, \qquad (3.1)$$

where

P_i = price of ith dwelling

$A_{i1}, A_{i2}, \ldots, A_{in}$ = quantities of attributes $1, 2, \ldots, n$ possessed by the ith dwelling

$a_1, a_2, \ldots, a_n$ = the implicit unit prices of A_1, $A_2, \ldots, A_n$.

As we have seen, in any given market the stock of housing will comprise a number of dwellings representing varying 'bundles' of attributes. The demand for different attributes, together with the supply of them, results in the determination of a set of attribute prices, $a_1, a_2, \ldots, a_n$. It is the estimation of these implicit prices within a particular local market which has been the aim of the majority of empirical work. When a well-defined estimate is obtained for a particular attribute price it is possible to gauge the importance of that attribute in the total property price, and also to make predictions about the way this price would change if the attribute mix were varied. However, it should always be borne in mind that these implicit prices are determined jointly by demand and supply conditions (that is, they are endogenous variables within the housing market) and it is to these conditions and their determinants that we must look ultimately for the cause of relative property prices.

Some Methodological Issues

To estimate a relationship of the type shown in equation (3.1) the most common method used has been ordinary least squares, multiple regression analysis. But this cannot be applied until a number of methodological issues have been resolved. First, as Ball and Kirwan (1975) point out, a straightforward additive form of relationship comprising distinct and independent attributes, such as that shown above, may not be an appropriate representation of the way that attributes are, in fact, combined. They put forward a possible alternative which involves two types of attributes: one distinct and additive, and another which exerts a multiplicative influence through attributes of the first type. This could be represented by an equation of the following form:

$$P_i = a_i(z_{i1}{}^{\lambda_1})A_{i1} + a_2(z_{i2}{}^{\lambda_2})A_2 + \ldots + a_n(z_{in}{}^{\lambda_n})A_n, \qquad (3.2)$$

where

$$z_{i1}, z_{i2}, \ldots, z_{in} = \text{attributes with multiplicative influences}$$

exerted on $A_{i1}, A_{i2}, \ldots, A_{in}$

$\lambda_1, \lambda_2, \ldots, \lambda_n = $ parameters.

In principle, the appropriate form of equation should be specified before estimation takes place, although in practice, data limitations often result in the same data set being used simultaneously to both select and test the equation form.

A second problem concerns the selection of a suitable sample of house prices and attributes for the econometric work. Price data are only readily available for houses at the time at which they are traded, but only a small proportion of the total housing stock within any area is usually traded each year. Therefore, if the whole stock is to be used as a sample frame, either house prices recorded at different dates in the past, or household valuations based on survey information, will have to be used. The former approach obviously introduces problems of comparability, whereas the latter suffers from the defect that, for various reasons, non-movers are likely to be in disequilibrium positions in relation to prevailing market prices.[7] For these reasons most studies confine their samples to recent movers.

A third problem that is often encountered in the estimation procedure is multicollinearity between the independent variables.

This occurs because certain attributes (or more precisely, attribute quantities) tend to be found together in similar types of dwellings. For example, a high-quality suburban dwelling will tend to have a large plot, a low density of occupation, central heating and other amenities, garage facilities, a clean environment, etc., whereas a poor-quality inner-city house will probably form a part of a high density development, have a large number of persons per room, lack certain basic amenities and be located in a poor environment. The correlations between attributes mean that it is not possible to distinguish the price associated with any single one of them. Faced with this problem, some researchers (for example, Kain and Quigley (1970), Wilkinson (1971a, 1973), Davies (1974)), have used principal component or factor analysis as a means of grouping attributes that are highly intercorrelated so that they may be expressed in terms of a single 'factor'. These factors can be interpreted as representing particular categories of housing services as they are perceived by consumers, for example, internal dwelling amenities, external dwelling amenities, socio-demographic composition of the neighbourhood. As the factors are generated from the data in such a way that they are uncorrelated with each other, they are able to be used as independent variables in the regression analysis.[8]

A final problem concerns possible variations in the same attribute price within a particular study area. This may arise if there are housing market imperfections which lead to the same attributes having different prices in separate sub-markets. Barriers to mobility experienced by certain slum area residents of the type discussed in Chapter Seven, which result in their paying higher prices per unit of slum housing than are paid for similar units of non-slum housing, represent one such imperfection. If these price variations do exist, and regression analysis is carried out on data combined from different sub-markets without any allowance being made for them, the parameter estimates obtained will be hybrid, area-wide averages rather than measures of actual prices. Ball and Kirwan (1977) test for the possibility of attribute price variations between owner-occupied sub-markets in the Bristol area by estimating separate house price equations for each sub-market, as well as an area-wide equation. The individual sub-market equations do not yield a well-defined set of separate attribute price estimates, nor do they reduce the proportion of over-all unexplained house price variation below that achieved in the area-wide equation. Consequently, Ball and Kirwan conclude that there is no evidence of the existence of separate sub-markets with individual price structures. However, it is probably fair to say that this subject requires more research before the intuitively plausible hypothesis of sub-market price variations is rejected.

Some Empirical Results

From the numerous results that have been produced by researchers investigating relative house prices, two subjects stand out as being of particular interest: these are the role of location and accessibility, and the relative importance of dwelling and environment attributes.

As we noted in Chapter One, the spatial character of the housing market is something that distinguishes it from most other markets. It is also a feature that has attracted the attention of a number of theorists. Their basic hypothesis is that households desire access to a range of activities, especially workplaces, and that as travel costs (in terms of both time and money) are an increasing function of residential distance from these activities, the price they will be willing to pay for an identical dwelling (that is, their 'bid' price) will vary inversely with its distance from these activities. Hence writers such as Alonso (1964), Wingo (1961) and Muth (1969) adopt the simplifying assumption that all non-residential activities are concentrated at the centre of a particular area, and then by using neo-classical, constrained utility maximisation models – in which the household is able to trade off housing space against travel costs – they are able to predict household residential site choices and a negatively sloped market land–price gradient radiating from the centre. Furthermore, if travel costs increase with distance at a *decreasing* rate, then these theories predict that the price of land will fall at a *decreasing* rate.

A substantial amount of empirical work has been devoted to testing these predictions; in particular, the expected negative slope and mathematical form of the price–distance gradient. Clark (1966) brings together the results of a number of studies carried out for some of the world's major cities, and confirms the expected negative correlation between land values and distance from the central business district (CBD). For Britain, Stone (1965) discovers a negative exponential relationship between the price per acre paid for building land and the distance from the centre of the region in both the London and Birmingham areas. Other studies have tested the theory by examining house price differentials on the assumption that location costs constitute one form of housing attribute expenditure. Wabe (1971), in his study of journeys to work in the London Metropolitan region, found the expected relationship between house prices and rail travel times and costs to the CBD, although his multiple regression analysis revealed correlations between location and other housing attributes, such as environmental quality, and thereby confirmed that the relationship is more complex than the simple distance–price trade-off theories are sometimes taken to imply. Evans (1973) sought to overcome the problem of variations in non-distance factors by selecting a sample of similar properties sharing the same generally high level of environmental quality, located on a radial line stretching from the centre of London. After this standardisation procedure had been carried out, he found that distance exerted the expected negative, non-linear effect and that it accounted for 74 per cent of the remaining price variation. Wilkinson (1974), on the other hand, pointed out that in many cities the classical price–distance relationship does not apply. He cited his study of Leeds as providing an example of a city in which there is easy access to the CBD from most locations. In consequence, relative access costs do not emerge as a significant house price determinant. A related complication arises in the case of multi-nucleated cities where workplaces and other activities are not all concentrated at the centre but are dispersed between the centre and a series of subcentres. Here the pattern of land use would tend to result in a price–distance gradient of the form indicated by curve *B* in Figure 3.5 rather than the more straightforward negative exponential form of curve *A*. One way of allowing for the effect of multiple-trip destinations is to construct some form of 'opportunity index' of the type used in transport studies. These measure accessibility from a given origin to all the destinations that a household may wish to visit and express it as a single, average index. The construction of such an index does, however, involve a number of conceptual problems which make the final interpretation of the distance 'effect' problematic.[9]

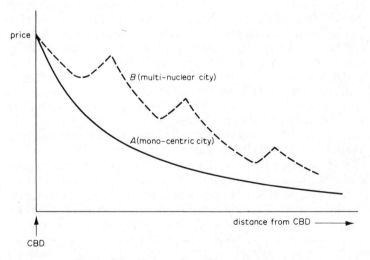

Figure 3.5   House price–distance gradients

On the question of the relative importance of dwelling attributes and their environmental surroundings, Kain and Quigley (1970), in their study of rented households in St Louis, found that factors representing 'basic residential quality' (BRQ) – which included the condition of drives and walks, landscaping, structural quality of adjoining dwellings, percentage of dwellings vacant, etc. – and other aspects of the neighbourhood environment such as the incidence of commercial and industrial land uses in the vicinity, accounted for nearly 25 per cent of the mean rental payment. They also found that home owners were willing to pay $1400 more for an otherwise comparable dwelling that was one standard deviation better than the average in terms of BRQ (although mean dwelling prices were not given, the relative importance of BRQ is indicated by the fact this sum is nearly twice as much as they were willing to pay for a dwelling that was one standard deviation better than the average in terms of the quality of the dwelling structure itself). The importance of environmental features is stressed even more strongly in Wilkinson's study of Leeds. On the basis of a sample of home owners who had recently bought their dwellings, he found that environmental factors representing the socio-economic composition of the area, the density of occupation, the gross residential density and other measures of area 'quality', were a more important source of house price variation than the features of the dwellings themselves. On the other hand, Ball and Kirwan, in their Bristol study, found that the physical dimensions of housing accounted for nearly 75 per cent of house price variation and that the addition of neighbourhood environmental factors added little to the explanatory power of their equations. There is, therefore, a certain amount of conflicting evidence on this subject. This may result from differences in study design, or it may, as Ball himself points out in another context (Ball, 1973), arise because of differences in demand and supply conditions between individual cities.

This completes our review of some of the models that have been used to provide an understanding of the way in which the housing market operates. It has shown how the determination of prices and the allocation of housing can be examined in terms of demand and supply analysis, but that the incorporation of the various complicating factors discussed in Chapter One suggests particular methodological approaches. But ultimately we are still concerned with demand and supply conditions, and consequently in the next two chapters a more detailed account of the demand for housing and its supply is presented.

CHAPTER FOUR

The Demand for Housing

In this chapter we shall concentrate on empirical studies of demand that have sought to identify the quantitative relationship between housing demand and its various determinants. These studies are of considerable practical importance because they provide the basis for forecasts of future housing requirements. As such, their approaches often differ according to whether they are designed to deal with short-run changes or the long-term future. If it is the short run that is of immediate concern, a study will usually tend to concentrate upon economic determinants of demand such as income, price and credit terms, assigning only a subsidiary role to socio-demographic factors. This emphasis is appropriate because it can usually be assumed that demographic factors will remain unchanged in the short run. Thus it is the impact of changes in income tax, credit availability, or of rent supplement schemes upon the existing population's housing demand which is of immediate interest to the Government's short-term policy advisers. In the long-term, however, the socio-demographic factors become important; indeed, they are often considered more important and predictable than most economic variables. Accordingly, in forecasting the emphasis shifts to projections of population, household formation rates, household size distributions, etc., and the housing requirements associated with them. Moreover, in many cases it has become the practice to use the concept of housing *need*, rather than demand, as the relevant measure of housing requirements. Here our main concern will be with those housing demand studies which stress conventional economic factors although, because of their widespread use in the area of long-term prediction, we have devoted the final section of this chapter to a discussion of the concept of housing need and some of the main features of projections using the concept.

As most of the econometric research on housing demand has been carried out in the United States, much of our discussion will reflect this North American emphasis (although a number of British studies that have appeared in recent years will also be examined). However, while we should obviously be wary of applying results obtained in another country to the British situation, these American studies are of considerable interest both because of the general magnitudes of the various demand elasticities they have identified and because of the methodological issues they highlight.

Methods of Analysis

For the most part, attention has been devoted to examining the relationship between housing demand and income, although the influences of price, credit terms and a range of household socio-economic characteristics have also been studied. Generally, multiple regression analysis has been used to estimate the precise quantitative relationship between demand – variously measured in terms of rent payments, imputed rent payments based on property values, or, sometimes, property capital values themselves[1] – and these explanatory variables. This has been applied at two main levels of aggregation: at the household level, using cross-sectional data obtained from sample surveys of consumers' expenditure, and at the national level, using time series data of national expenditure aggregates.

Once an equation has been estimated on the basis of sample data[2], the individual coefficient (parameter) estimates will indicate how demand can be expected to respond to changes in the explanatory variables. That is, they provide the basis for calculating measures of demand elasticity. For example, if a relationship of the linear form illustrated in equation (4.1) is used,

$$h = b_0 + b_1 y + b_2 p + b_3 i, \qquad (4.1)$$

where h = housing demand, y = income, p = price, i = the mortgage interest rate, and the bs are the parameters associated with each variable, then the income elasticity of demand at any point on the function can be obtained by differentiating the function with respect to income and combining this result with the h and y variable values at the relevant point. That is,

$$e_{hy} = \frac{\partial h}{\partial y} \cdot \frac{y}{h} = b_1 \cdot \frac{y}{h} \qquad (4.2)$$

Other demand elasticities may, of course, be obtained from equation (4.1) by a similar process. Thus the price elasticity of demand may be expressed as follows:

$$e_{hp} = \frac{\partial h}{\partial p} \cdot \frac{p}{h} = b_2 \cdot \frac{p}{h} \qquad (4.3)$$

In both of the above instances, however, the elasticity measures will vary over the range of the function because it is linear whereas the elasticity of demand refers to proportionate changes. When confronted with this type of variability, it is a common procedure to express the results obtained in terms of the elasticity at the point of sample means. Thus equation (4.2) would show the income elasticity of demand at the mean income $(\bar{y})$ level:

$$e_{hy} = \frac{\partial h}{\partial y} \cdot \frac{\bar{y}}{\bar{h}}. \tag{4.4}$$

On other occasions, it is sometimes felt that a multiplicative relationship of the form shown in equation (4.5) is a better representation of the way in which the explanatory variables determine housing demand than the linear form of equation presented in (4.1):

$$h = d_0 y^{d_1} \cdot p^{d_2} \cdot i^{d_3}, \tag{4.5}$$

where h, p and i are as defined above, and the ds are the parameters. This functional form can be converted into a linear equation suitable for estimation by standard multiple regression techniques, by the simple device of expressing it in logarithmic form. Thus, equation (4.5) becomes:

$$\log h = d_0 + d_1 \log y + d_2 \log p + d_3 \log i. \tag{4.6}$$

Moreover, the multiplicative (or log-linear) form has the added attraction that its elasticity measures remain constant over its entire range and can, furthermore, be observed directly. That is, the income elasticity of demand can be shown to be equal to the value of the income variable's parameter, d_1; similarly the price elasticity can be shown to be equal to d_2, and so on[3].

Having now discussed briefly the way in which demand elasticities may be estimated from two commonly used functional forms, we shall proceed to consider some specific studies and the results they have obtained.

Housing and Income: Cross-section Household Studies

Most of the very early European investigations of housing conditions during the nineteenth and early twentieth centuries concurred with Schwabe's law of rent which suggested that the proportion of income devoted to housing fell as household income rose.[4] These observations implied an income elasticity of housing demand of less than one and were consistent with the view of housing as a 'necessity'.

There was, however, one eminent dissenter from this view: the English economist Alfred Marshall wrote: 'houseroom satisfies the imperative need for shelter, but that need plays little part in the effective demand for houseroom' and 'where the condition of society is healthy, and there is no check on general prosperity, there seems always to be an elastic demand for houseroom, on account of the real conveniences and social distinction it affords'.[5]

Evidence from the United States

Even so, contrary to Marshall's belief, the work of the early modern American researchers seemed to support the former view of an inelastic demand. For example, Maisel and Winnick (1960) working with consumer expenditure sample survey data for 1950, stratified by occupation, education, family size, age of household head and residential location (and thus standardised for possible variations in expenditure patterns resulting from these factors), obtained income elasticity measures in the range 0.49 to 0.72. Lee (1963), working with a rather different model, also found demand to be relatively inelastic. Using data obtained in the 1958 Michigan Survey of Consumer Finances, he developed and tested a model in which decisions affecting house purchase were looked at in a four-stage, ordered sequence, that is, the probability of buying a house, the price to be paid, the probability of obtaining mortgage debt, and the amount of debt obtained. The second stage of this model, which identified income as one of the significant determinants of the house purchase price, yielded an income elasticity measure of 0.89. While this estimate was above those obtained by Maisel and Winnick it was still below unity.

However, with the publication of Margaret Reid's monumental study in 1962, work on the subject took a new direction. Reid argued that decisions regarding housing expenditure are viewed over a longer time period than multiple correlation analysis using *current* income and housing expenditure had hitherto suggested. Because of the inconvenience of moving house and the considerable transactions costs involved, housing consumption will not be adjusted frequently; instead there will be periodic adjustments that will depend not only on current income, but past and expected future income streams as well. For this reason the concept of permanent or normal income as developed by Friedman (1957) was thought to be the relevant measure for determining family housing expenditure. Moreover the permanent income elasticity of housing demand may be expected to have a higher value than those obtained using current income. Why this should be so can be seen by considering the permanent income hypothesis.

Friedman maintained that measured or current income (Y) will comprise two distinct components: permanent income (Y_p), which is the individual's long-run anticipated income based on past earnings and expectations about the future, and transitory income (Y_t) which causes unforeseen short-run aberrations from the long-run trend. The transitory component may be either positive or negative but will not be expected to persist. Loss of earnings through temporary short-time working or a Christmas bonus payment would represent examples of transitory income. Housing expenditure (H) can be expected to be related to permanent income but not to transitory income.[6] Now if, as is likely, households receiving above average incomes tend to have positive transitory income, whereas households with below average incomes experience negative transitory income, housing expenditure in relation to current income will be higher for the low-income households, and lower for the high-income households, than it would be in relation to each group's permanent income. Thus any elasticity measure obtained from the relationship between housing expenditure and current income will underestimate the permanent income elasticity. Figure 4.1 illustrates this point.

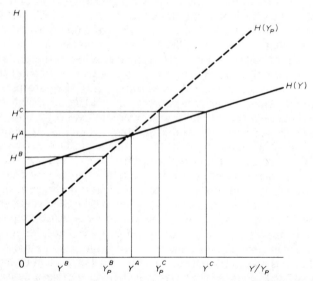

Figure 4.1   Permanent income and housing consumption

The schedule $H(Y_p)$ represents the relationship between housing consumption and permanent income for a sample of households at a given time. The proportion of income devoted to housing expenditure rises as household permanent income rises. $H(Y)$, on the other hand, is a schedule that might be expected to be estimated on the basis of observations of household housing expenditure and current income. For purposes of illustration, let us consider the behaviour of three households that would produce such a schedule. Household A receives the sample average income so that its transitory income is zero and, therefore, current income equals permanent income. Hence its income-expenditure combination, $0\,Y^A(\,=\,0\,Y_p^A)/0H^A$, lies on both $H(Y_p)$ and $H(Y)$. Household B, on the other hand, has a permanent income of $0\,Y_p^B$ which is greater than its current income because of a negative transitory component. However, this transitory component does not affect its housing consumption and it continues to consume $0H^B$. Conversely, household C has a permanent income of Y_p^C which is below its current income of $0\,Y^C$ because of a positive transitory component. But, once again, this does not affect its housing consumption – this remains a function of permanent income. Thus the presence of either positive or negative transitory income will tend to produce an observed housing expenditure-current income function, $H(Y)$, which is less elastic than the permanent income function.

As most of the survey data on consumers' income used in the earlier studies was likely to have contained large elements of transitory income, the elasticity measures obtained would have underestimated the permanent income elasticity. Reid sought to correct for this bias by taking average household income and expenditure measures for a sample of different areas. In this way it was hoped that the individual transitory income components of households within each area would be self-cancelling and that the resulting averages would approximate the permanent income level for each area. Both average city income and expenditure, for a sample of cities, and census tract averages within the same city were used at different stages in the analysis. The results suggested a permanent income elasticity of demand for home owners in the range 1.5 to 2.0; a measure that was substantially above those previously obtained and which implied that a greater proportion of income was devoted to housing expenditure as income rose. For renters, the elasticity measures were somewhat lower, ranging from 0.8 to 1.2, but these were still higher than earlier studies had suggested. (To a certain extent one would expect the elasticity to be higher for owners than for renters as they have a wider choice of housing and are therefore able to adjust their expenditures to obtain accommodation of their choosing somewhat more easily. Furthermore, Reid felt that the incidence of rent control in many areas tended to produce a downward bias in the renters' elasticity measures by depressing housing expenditure figures.)

Reid's findings were supported by Muth (1960) who in the process of conducting a more extensive time series study (see next section) also included a cross section analysis of house values in relation to permanent income. On the basis of sample city averages for 1950, his work suggested a permanent income elasticity of 1.7.

Subsequent research has, however, suggested that the Reid and Muth results may have overestimated the permanent income elasticity. A second study by Lee (1968) used data for three separate years, 1960–2, collected by the Michigan Survey of Consumer Finances. On the basis of the three sets of observations he computed permanent income figures for individual households and thereby avoided the need to resort to averaging. His results produced substantially lower elasticity estimates; 0.8 for home owners and 0.7 for renters. Lee believed that part of the reason for the difference between his own and Reid's estimates was due to upward bias in her intra-city results introduced by her averaging procedure. He claimed that there was a correlation between the census tracts over which households were averaged and certain housing qualitative features. This led to households with strong preferences for housing (relative to other goods and services) being found in different census areas to those with weak preferences, even though they had similar income levels. Thus a 'preference' effect was identified as an 'income' effect. But as DeLeeuw (1971) later pointed out it was likely that Lee's results were also biased, but in the opposite direction, because his sample excluded households that moved during the three-year survey period. As moving from one dwelling to another is the major means of adjusting housing expenditure (DeLeeuw claimed that approximately 50 per cent of renter housesholds moved every two years),[7] it is probable that a sample which omits recent movers will under-represent those households who are actively adjusting their expenditure.

Another study that raised doubts about the procedures adopted by Reid was conducted by Winger (1968). He felt that Reid's results were likely to have produced overestimates of the income elasticity of demand because she had not taken account of mortgage credit. Because access to credit is likely to increase as income increases, its influence will be identified as an income effect, unless an explicit credit variable is included in the regression equations. In his own study, Winger used data on house purchase values and incomes provided by the Federal Housing Administration (FHA) for those properties on which it had advanced loans. Because the terms on which the Agency lends money tend to be broadly the same for all borrowers (a 95 per cent loan-to-value ratio and repayments over thirty years), Winger argued that the credit effect would be standardised within his sample. After allowing for this effect, his regressions of house value on income suggested an income elasticity of approximately one, which is again a great deal lower than those estimated by Reid and Muth.

However, as in the case of Lee's work, DeLeeuw, in the article referred to previously, suggested that Winger's results may also have underestimated the population elasticity because of the special features of his sample. In particular, DeLeeuw pointed out that FHA loans were restricted to purchases of houses in the middle-value range. Both high- and low-valued properties were excluded. This meant that some households receiving low incomes, who might be expected to buy low-valued properties below the minimum at which an FHA loan would be forthcoming, would 'overspend' in order to qualify for a loan. Conversely, some households on higher incomes would moderate their expenditure and buy cheaper property in order to qualify for a loan. This over- and under-spending at each end of the income distribution would tend to distort the observed income elasticity. On the basis of 1969 Census data of FHA- and non-FHA-assisted housing groups, DeLeeuw suggested that Winger's results should be adjusted upwards by as much as 50 per cent to compensate for this effect.

In fact, DeLeeuw reviewed all four of the studies mentioned so far – those of Reid, Muth, Lee and Winger – and argued that the discrepancies between their results would be reduced if each of them was corrected for (i) the distinction between housing value and annual housing expenses as a measure of housing consumption, (ii) their omission of the imputed rent income received by home owners and (iii) sampling problems which sometimes made the data unrepresentative of the general population they purported to represent. Regarding the first point, the distinction between house value and annual expenses is important because annual expenses (which will include insurance, maintenance and repairs, etc., as well as loan interest and repayments) tend to represent a declining proportion of value as value rises. Hence estimates of elasticity based on value need to be adjusted downwards if they are to be compared with estimates based on expenses. Second, the inclusion of imputed income is necessary because it can be shown that if it is omitted, elasticity measures of less than one will be biased downwards, and measures greater than one will be biased upwards.[8] Finally, the representativeness of the sample is important for the reasons mentioned already. When the results obtained from each of the four studies had been adjusted to allow for these factors, the dispersion of elasticity measures that had extended from 0.6 to 2.1 was reduced to 0.7 to 1.5 (0.8 to 1.0 for renters, and 0.7 to 1.5 for home owners). In addition, DeLeeuw himself supplemented these findings with some of his own based on median housing expenditure and income data for nineteen metropolitan areas in 1960. Both the renter and home-owner elasticity measures fell comfortably in the above range with values of slightly under and over one, for each group respectively.

Finally, two recent studies reported by Maisel (1971) and Carliner (1973) show that equations estimated on the basis of individual household data will produce lower elasticity estimates than those obtained from the same data if they are used after they have been grouped and averaged.[9] Among other things, this probably explains why Lee's results tend to be somewhat lower than the others considered by DeLeeuw. In his work Maisel obtains an elasticity measure of 0.45 from a sample of 2900 new home purchases insured by the FHA in 1966. Carliner, using Michigan Survey research material, obtains estimates of 0.6 to 0.7 for owners and 0.5 for renters. Thus both of them support the earlier view of an income elasticity of demand that is well below unity.

To conclude this section let us, by way of summary, try to identify some of the main points that emerge from this body of American evidence. First, we can see very clearly that there is no single estimate of the income elasticity of demand for housing available; indeed, it is not even possible to answer the original question of whether it is greater or less than unity. Furthermore the range of estimates is rather large, extending from 0.5 to 1.5. However, on the positive side, our knowledge of the estimates observed when a variety of procedures have been followed does allow us to identify some important sources of variation. First, we know that differing results will be obtained according to the equation and variable specifications used. Notably, the use of permanent income will produce a higher estimate than the use of current income. Second, a range of problems – and the biases they are likely to introduce if not overcome – associated with sampling procedures have been highlighted. Third, we know that the level of aggregation at which the analysis is conducted will affect the elasticity measures obtained; specifically, grouped data will yield higher estimates than ungrouped data. And, finally, most of the studies show that the income elasticity of demand for renter households is below that of owners.

Evidence from Britain

In comparison with the United States there has been far less econometric research on the relationship between housing expenditure and income carried out in Britain. One reason for this is, no doubt, data limitations. For example, consumer expenditure sample surveys of the type carried out by the University of Michigan have been far less common in Britain, although the *Family Expenditure Survey* (FES) now conducted annually by the government provides one recent exception. However, another reason for the lack of British research in this area is probably the nature of the British housing market. In particular, the existence of a substantial housing sector in which market forces are either subject to stringent regulation (for example, rent-controlled or regulated properties) or where the price system has been largely replaced by other allocational devices (such as Local Authority Housing). In these sectors the relationship between the amount spent on housing and the quantity of housing consumed is very different to that observed in an unregulated market and, in consequence, conventional demand elasticity measures are far less appropriate. Moreover, the supply constraints operating within these sectors are often more rigid than those in the owner-occupied sector and thus make it more difficult for households to adjust their demand by moving to larger or smaller homes. Observed demand elasticity will therefore be far less pronounced.

None the less, despite these difficulties, a number of studies have appeared in recent years as interest in housing policy issues has grown among economists. One of the first of these was carried out by Clark and Jones (1971). They used data collected through the FES for the years 1966 and 1967 to examine the relationship between housing and income. The FES is an official annual sample survey of the expenditure patterns of approximately eleven thousand households. It records weekly payments associated with housing – such as rent, rates, maintenance and repair work – as well as other items in the family budget. In the case of owner-occupier households, where no actual rent payments are made, an imputed figure based upon the rateable value of the property is recorded. The survey does not include estimates of permanent income and so in their analysis Clark and Jones used total household expenditure as a proxy for permanent income on the assumption that this would not fluctuate erratically in response to changes in transitory income. It is, therefore, likely to be a superior surrogate to reported current income. Using this 'permanent income' measure and various alternative measures of housing expenditure, they first of all analysed households in the three main tenure categories separately, and termed it a 'tenure-confined' analysis. They found that the income elasticity of demand for owner-occupier and private (unfurnished) tenants was slightly below unity, whereas, as one would expect, the lower prices and tight supply constraints in the LA sector produced a substantially lower elasticity measure of 0.4. Taken together the tenure-confined elasticities yielded an all-group weighted average value of 0.85.

However, recognising that one of the main ways in which British households upgrade their housing demand is to change tenure categories – in particular to become owner-occupiers – they also computed elasticity measures on a 'tenure-free' basis. This increased the all-group weighted average to 0.95. They felt, however, that this small increase over the tenure-confined measure was probably an underestimate, possibly because the expenditure figures for owner-occupiers, which were based upon property rateable values, understated their actual expenditure. Also, the qualitative superiority of owner-occupied housing tends to be represented inadequately by its rateable value. If adjustments for these factors were made, elasticity measures of up to 1.5 would be feasible.

Vipond and Walker (1972) also used FES data in their study. They began by looking at housing expenditure in relation to current income and found very low elasticity measures of between 0.1 and 0.2. When they too used total expenditure as a proxy for permanent income, their estimates were increased to 0.4–0.5, but still remained below those obtained by Clark and Jones. They attributed the difference to the fact that Clark and Jones had been able to standardise their data for other factors likely to influence housing expenditure, such as the age of the head of the household (which is an indication of the stage the household has reached in its life-cycle), whereas because of data limitations they were unable to do so.

Byatt, Holmans and Laidler (1973) report on some of the research on housing demand carried out within the Department of the Environment (DOE). To study the demand by home owners they were able to use two separate sets of survey data: the first was a 5 per cent sample survey of building society mortgages which has been carried out regularly by the DOE since 1966. It records the purchase price of a mortgaged property, the amount and rate of interest charged on the mortgage, as well as the purchaser's income, his age, sex and previous tenure. The second data source was a special survey of mortgage loans granted by the Abbey National Building Society in February 1970. This produced 2 800 usable replies and provided rather more detailed information about borrowers than the first survey. In particular, it included personal details that enabled the borrower's after-tax income to be calculated, and also the selling price of his previous home. The latter piece of information indicated his access to liquid assets. By choosing to use building society data on mortgages the authors recognised that they were concentrating on households who were actually in the process of moving and, as we have seen, it could be argued that such households are not representative of the general population. However, a counter argument put forward by Byatt *et al.* in favour of this procedure maintains that 'there are likely to be long lags (and on occasion long leads) in the adjustment of housing to changes in income and other circumstances.

A move is an opportunity to adjust housing consumption to income, among other variables, and thus provides a particularly suitable opportunity for observing households' underlying behavioural relationships'.[10]

On the basis of these data the authors obtained income elasticity of demand estimates of 0.6 to 0.7; however, they had a number of reasons for suspecting bias in these results. For example, the available data meant that current income (after tax payments) had to be used as the independent variable rather than permanent income or some proxy for it. They therefore devoted considerable attention to the task of specifying the possible extent of this bias on the basis of plausible assumptions about the variance of measurement errors. After allowing for various possibilities they concluded that the true elasticity was likely to lie in the range 0.75 to 1.0.

They also examined the demand for housing by private tenants in uncontrolled property on the basis of FES data for 1965 and 1968 (rent-controlled tenants were excluded because of the distortions produced in the consumption-rent relationship which were mentioned earlier). In this analysis they were able to use total household expenditure on non-durable goods as a surrogate for permanent income. (Expenditure on durable goods was excluded because it was thought that purchases of these items were more likely to respond to changes in transitory income.) The results supported the American evidence by suggesting somewhat lower income elasticities than those obtained for home owners.

Thus the British evidence amassed to date is certainly consistent with that obtained in the United States. For home owners an income elasticity of between 0.75 and 1.0 appears likely, although it may be as large as 1.5 if adjustments for qualitative features and other factors considered by Clark and Jones are made.

Housing and Income: Aggregate Time-series Analysis

There has been a large amount of work carried out on the macro-economics of housing demand, mainly in the form of investment expenditure models. Some of these have considered housing in its own right while others have dealt with it as a part of a larger model of the overall economy. As we are concerned primarily with the micro-economic aspects of the housing market, we shall not be commenting on this work here.[11] However, we have included one such model below, because it makes use of a capital stock adjustment model similar to the one we presented in the previous chapter, which shows the crucial role of changes through time in the housing market. This is the model developed by Muth (1960).

Muth postulated that at any point in time there will be a desired stock of housing which will be demanded for the flow of services it provides per unit of time. The size of this desired-stock (h^*) will depend upon the price of housing (p), permanent income (y) and the mortgage rate of interest (i). Formally, this can be expressed in a linear form as:

$$h^* = b_0 + b_1 p + b_2 y + b_3 i. \tag{4.7}$$

If in any period a discrepancy between the size of the desired-stock and the actual stock (h) occurs, there will be a tendency for the actual stock to adjust towards the desired level. (Muth considers the process of change working through the level of rent payments (r) made for housing services. Thus if $h^* > h$, a greater quantity of housing services will be demanded at the market rent than are available, hence the rent will be bid up. If the supply price of housing (p) is cost-determined this will remain unchanged and so the rate of return on housing (r/p) will rise above its long-run equilibrium level, which occurs when $h^* = h$, presenting an incentive to increase the size of the stock.) The adjustment process may be represented as follows:

$$\Delta h = d(h^* - h), \tag{4.8}$$

where Δh = the increase in the stock per period, and d = an adjustment factor. Because of both demand and supply side response lags, it is unlikely that the difference between h^* and h will be eliminated within a single period and therefore d will tend to be less than one. (On the basis of annual data, Muth calculated that $d = 0.3$, which suggests that 30 per cent of any shortfall will be eliminated each year.)

Now within the Muth model it is the *desired-stock* income elasticity of demand that is of interest because this is the variable which is the basis of the behavioural relationship: the target towards which the actual stock of housing will move. Hence an estimate of $\dfrac{\partial h^*}{\partial y} \dfrac{y}{h^*}$ is required. However, it is not possible to estimate this term straightforwardly from equation (4.7) because the variable h^* is not directly observable. However, by using a substitution process, Muth shows how the required elasticity can in fact be calculated.[12] His results indicate a permanent income, desired-stock elasticity of demand of 0.88. Extensive experimentation with the basic form showed that if the lagged adjustment process had been neglected (that is, if it were assumed that the actual stock of housing adjusted to the desired stock within a single period of time), a substantially lower elasticity estimate would have been obtained. This would arise because the 'carry-over' or long-term influence of a change in income taking place in the second and subsequent periods would have been ignored.

Following the Muth tradition, an important pioneering study was carried out recently in Britain by Whitehead (1971, 1974). She also used a desired-stock adjustment formulation which was tested on aggregate quarterly time series data for the years 1955–70. In addition, however, Whitehead specified the formulation as part of a three-equation model designed to take account of the joint nature of the determination of demand, supply, price, etc. The first equation expressed demand as a function of income, price, mortgage rates and expected future prices – to allow for the investment motive in house purchase decisions. (The form was similar to equation (A) in note 12.) The second equation expressed the supply of new housing (in terms of housing 'starts') as a function of house prices, building costs and the cost of credit to builders. Finally, the third equation specified a lag structure between the supply of 'starts' and the supply of completed new houses. The various coefficients in each of these equations were estimated by two-stage, least-squares regression techniques which take account of the simultaneity of determination. The results yielded very low estimates of the income elasticity of demand, indicating values in the range 0.01 to 0.56. However, several features of Whitehead's approach mean that they are not strictly comparable with either the Muth or the cross-sectional results cited earlier. For example, because of data limitations, Whitehead used the number of dwellings as a measure of demand, rather than expenditure or value measures. Similar data inadequacies also prevented the use of a permanent income variable. Taken together, these limitations suggest that Whitehead's study is probably of more interest for the methodological issues it identifies than for the precise results it yields.

Price and Credit

In the process of looking at the relationship between income and housing demand we have seen that most studies have employed multivariate techniques of analysis which allow them to take account of other determinants of housing demand. Among these other determinants, price and the cost (and/or availability) of credit often figure prominently.

Price

As in the case of most commodities, we would expect to find that the quantity of housing demanded will depend upon its price, especially as housing expenditure accounts for up to one-third of the average household's budget. Estimation of the precise form of the price–quantity relationship is, however, often hampered by problems associated with the observation and measurement of price variations. These make the calculation of elasticity measures more difficult than in the case of income. Nevertheless, cross-sectional analysis is sometimes possible when there is a sample of areas in which the price of housing varies between individual areas because of differing land and/or construction costs. Thus cities with different price structures sometimes provide the opportunity for observing variations in the quantities of housing demanded by households at different price levels. For aggregate time series analysis to be possible, it is necessary to measure the movements in the price of housing relative to the prices of other goods and services (that is, the all-items retail price index). If, as a result of greater or slower than average rate of growth in building costs, these price movements display sufficient variability, they may enable the identification of the price–quantity relationship.

On the basis of one or other of these approaches, American studies carried out by Muth (1960), Maisel (1971) and DeLeeuw (1971) suggest that the price elasticity of demand is probably in the region of − 1.0, although the confidence interval surrounding this estimate is generally thought to be rather wide. (DeLeeuw, for example, estimated that the elasticity measure lies in the range − 0.7 to − 1.5.) If, however, the unit price elasticity measure is accepted as broadly correct, it implies that, *ceteris paribus*, a constant money expenditure tends to be devoted to housing. Thus if there is either an increase or a decrease in its price, there will be a compensating change (that is, a proportionate change in the opposite direction) in the quantity demanded. Compared with the United States, there is at present little evidence on the price elasticity of demand in the British market. The evidence which is available (Clark and Jones, 1971) suggests that demand is probably considerably more inelastic than in America. Estimates of − 0.6 and below have been put forward. *A priori* expectations would, of course, lead us to expect a greater degree of inelasticity in the British market because the existence of numerous supply constraints will reduce the scope for adjusting housing consumption in the face of price changes.

Credit

The discussion in Chapter One indicated the importance of long-term credit in the housing market – a market where relatively few households are in a position to buy property outright from their income and accumulated savings. The Department of the Environment's National Movers Survey showed that in 1973 approximately 85 per cent of buyers financed their purchases at least partly with a loan. Consequently the terms on which this credit is made available can have a considerable impact upon housing demand.

Consideration of the terms on which credit is offered by the main lending institutions – notably the Building Societies – suggests that a distinction should be drawn between price and non-price methods of rationing. The major instrument of price rationing is the interest rate charged to borrowers, although the actual monthly sum that the household has to repay will also depend upon the number of years over which the loan is extended. Most loans are scheduled for repayment over periods up to twenty-five years but longer periods, or extensions following increases in the interest rate, are often granted. (The declining real value of constant money repayments resulting from such long repayment periods in times of general inflation has led to a number of proposals for the reform of housing finance arrangements. In particular, methods that would give households presently on low incomes, but anticipating increases through their working lives, the opportunity to shift some of the early repayments burden into the future, have been widely canvassed (for example, Black, 1974).) Non-price rationing takes the form of decisions about whether or not an institution will lend to an individual or on a property, and the loan-to-value ratio it will offer (see Chapter One). In times of stringent credit rationing even low-risk applicants who satisfy the institutions' general requirements, and would be willing to pay above the market rate of interest to secure a loan, will usually find that credit is simply not available. In such times it is allocated through queueing rather than price.

For an area which has such an important role in the housing market there have been surprisingly few economic studies investigating the overall effect of the price of credit and its availability on the demand for housing. (On the other hand, there has been no shortage of casual comment on the role played by building society credit, especially in the period of major house price inflation between 1971 and 1973. There have also been a number of studies investigating the role of finance in particular local markets carried out by non-economists, for example, Harloe *et al.* (1974).) Those studies which have been undertaken suggest that non-price methods of rationing have been a more important determinant of demand than the cost of credit. For example, Gelfand (1966) examined the relative importance of the interest rate, the length of repayment period and the loan-to-value ratio for a sample of 1500 households in the state of Pennsylvania. He concluded that the down-payment requirement arising from loan-to-value lending practices was quantitatively the most important factor restricting households in their quest for housing of their choice. In Britain similar lending practices result in the households' liquidity position becoming an important determinant of demand. This factor was emphasised in the study of Byatt *et al.*, referred to earlier.

At the macro-level Guttentag (1961) has claimed that in the United States credit availability is *the* major determinant of short-term housing demand. Attempts to measure its influence in Britain have included Whitehead's use of a 'net flow-of-funds into building societies' variable – which assumes that this will dictate the amount they are able to loan – and O'Herlihy and Spencer's dummy variables which reflect periods of 'mild' and 'strict' rationing (O'Herlihy and Spencer, 1972). Although Whitehead's results are not conclusive they also point to the major role played by non-price credit rationing.

Forecasting Housing Demand

The foregoing discussion has shown that in recent years considerable progress has been made in econometric research on the demand for housing. We are still, however, a long way from the situation where all that is required to forecast housing demand is a formal model in which the expected future values of the explanatory variables can be simply 'plugged in' and the associated demand forecast duly 'cranked-out'. At present forecasting remains a far more eclectic exercise. A typical forecast will employ a range of techniques: some of these will involve formal econometric procedures whereas others will rely more heavily upon *ad hoc* judgements made by the forecasters. One example of such an approach is provided by Holmans (1970).

In his study, Holmans presents a disaggregated forecast of the effective demand for new housing over a medium-term period of ten years 1971–81. Among the features of particular interest in this study is the treatment of the relationship between demand in the different tenure categories which, as we have seen, is from the forecaster's point of view, a source of considerable complexity in the British market. Also the length of the forecast period is sufficiently long to expect changes in both demographic and economic factors to influence the level of housing demand. Accordingly, he starts by forecasting the demographic determinants of demand such as the number of new households expected to be formed, the numbers likely to be dissolved by death and other factors, and the number of immigrant households. Each of these is estimated on the basis of the Registrar-General's 1968 projections (supplemented by various other *ad hoc* sources of information) using the methodology described in the final section of this chapter. To obtain a forecast of effective demand (as distinct from need), these expectations about population characteristics are combined with data on key economic variables. Thus a number of assumptions about the rate of growth of income, house prices and mortgage interest rates over the decade are made. (In the event these assumptions seriously understated the price and earnings movements that actually occurred in the early 1970s – but, to be fair, this was true of most forecasts made at this time.) Having specified what seemed to be a plausible time profile for these demographic and economic factors, Holmans then used this information to forecast the three main components of housing demand. These were the demand from new households, the demand from movers between tenure groups and the demand from existing households within a particular tenure group[13]. Table 4.1 shows the components of demand and supply as estimated by Holmans for one tenure group, that is, owner-occupiers. Similar methods were used to predict demand in the LA and private rented sector to obtain an aggregate forecast of housing demand.

In the owner-occupied sector the tendency for average incomes to rise was expected to lead to a higher proportion of new households becoming home-owners than had been the case hitherto. This growth was expected to be largely at the expense of the private rental sector. Movements on the part of existing households from the LA and private rental sectors were predicted in terms of the income changes and relative price movements expected in each tenure category. Moreover the effect of anticipated government slum clearance schemes added to the expected demands from this source. Finally, the demands emanating from existing home-owners for new dwellings or second homes was forecast on the basis of an income elasticity of demand of 0.7 and a price elasticity of -0.3. In addition, the demands from this group were expected to be related to the capital gains they were likely to realise through house price inflation (that is, their liquidity position) and the greater propensity for the growing numbers of professional groups to consume more housing. Taken together, these components indicated the total demand for new housing in the owner-occupied sector which, when compared with the number of units expected to be vacated in the existing stock (see the second half of Table 4.1), showed the demands likely to be placed on the construction industry.

Housing Need and Long-term Projections

Housing need may be defined as the quantity of housing that is required to provide accommodation of an agreed minimum standard and above for a population given its size, household composition, age

TABLE 4.1
Components of supply and demand for owner-occupied housing

	thousands		
	1971	1976	1981
DEMAND			
1. New households	160	185	205
2. Former LA tenants	52	56	60
3. Former private tenants	145	135	125
4. Immigrants	13	12	12
Total first-time buyers	370	388	402
5. New houses for existing owners	123	124	121
6. Second dwellings	10	10	10
TOTAL	503	522	533
SUPPLY (from existing stock)			
7. Houses vacated by: households dissolved	73	81	88
8. emigrant households	33	30	30
9. h/hlds moving to LA sector	21	24–35	25–36
10. h/hlds moving to private renting	20	20	20
11. O/O moving to new houses	123	124	121
12. Houses formerly rented	75	65	65
TOTAL	345	344–355	349–360
13. Less: losses through slum-clearance	25	31–44	33–48
TOTAL SUPPLY FROM EXISTING STOCK	320	313–311	316–312

Source: Holmans (1970), table VII, p. 40.

distribution, etc., *without taking into account the individual household's ability to pay for the housing assigned to it.* Because of this last condition, need is sometimes described as a 'social' concept which is independent of economic considerations. This, however, is not strictly correct, for both the agreed standard of housing and, to a lesser extent, total housing requirements are dependent upon economic factors. For example, the standard of housing will depend, among other things, on what a society believes it can realistically achieve given its productive potential. Similarly, total housing requirements will depend upon the rate at which new households form, which in turn will frequently depend upon household income levels, particularly in relation to the price of housing. Nevertheless, although economic considerations underlie the concept of need, a housing need forecast will not assign a prominent role to them in the way that a demand forecast does. Moreover, because housing need is not based upon the individual household's ability to pay for the housing allocated to it, it represents society's view about the quantity and quality of housing that its members *should* receive. Thus a need projection differs from a demand forecast in that it is a statement of what is required to be provided, given expected future developments in population size and structure, instead of a prediction of what is expected to happen in response to income and price changes. And finally, because population trends change more slowly and predictably than the economic variables which determine demand, need projections tend to be made for considerably longer periods; time horizons of twenty to forty years are quite common.

A typical need projection may be conveniently divided into two parts: one part deals with population changes over the period in question and the other considers the stock of dwellings necessary to accommodate the forecast population. Then the second part, together with information about the existing stock of dwellings, indicates the number of additional dwellings required. Let us consider some of the main features of each of these stages.

The population projection will, first of all, require an estimate of the *total* population at different points in time throughout the forecast period. In Britain these projections are prepared annually by the Office of the Registrar-General. They are based on three main factors: the rates of deaths, births and international migration. In all these cases, past trends form the basis for extrapolation into the future. For example, death rates have in the past shown a systematic tendency to decline for all age groups and it is usually assumed that this trend will continue, at least into the foreseeable future. Birth rates – which, in turn, depend upon marriage rates, the age at which marriage takes place and preferences regarding family size – have tended to behave rather more erratically. The long-run decline from a peak of 35 births per thousand population which began in the 1870s continued, with short-term disturbances associated with the two world wars, until a figure of 15 per thousand was reached in 1955; thereafter the rate increased again until 1964 (19 per thousand), but has subsequently declined once more. Migration rates have fluctuated even more widely than birth rates. Recent experience shows that Britain was a net loser of population until the influx of Commonwealth immigrants of the late 1950s and early 1960s. Since that time the Commonwealth Immigration Act has reduced the flow of immigrants into the country, until by 1964 Britain was once again a net exporter of population. Obviously the larger the fluctuations in past birth and migration rates, the greater the degree of uncertainty surrounding forecasts. One method that some planners have adopted to give explicit recognition to this problem is to specify both 'high' and 'low' estimates, as well as a central forecast, to demonstrate the implications of either greater or smaller population growth.

Once the total population has been forecast it is necessary to estimate the number of separate households that it will contain, for it is the household which constitutes the basic unit requiring housing. This is usually done by breaking down the total population into separate categories based on age, sex and marital status, and then applying the appropriate household 'headship' rate to each category: that is, the proportion of each group that is expected to be a household head. Interestingly, evidence on headship rates for each of these categories in the past suggests that they have remained fairly stable even though changes in demographic patterns have led to changes in the relative sizes of the categories. However, it is likely that in the future there will be some increase in these rates as increased prosperity and earlier marriage, together with the easing of supply constraints arising from housing shortages, exert their influence on the rate of household formation.

The final stage of the population projection procedure is to estimate the household size distribution as this will determine the type of housing required. Once again information about the existing family size distribution, which is given in the population census, provides a starting point for a forecast. Clearly, family sizes will tend to vary according to the age and marital status of the head and so forecasts of changes in these population characteristics will carry with them implications for the family size distribution.[14] In addition, however, any expectations about family size changes resulting from changes in fertility, preferences regarding child-rearing, etc., must be added to these.

After the number of households and their size distribution has been forecast, the second part of the exercise requires an estimate of the stock and size distribution of dwellings necessary to house them. It is at this stage that decisions have to be made concerning the standard of housing that should be provided. Even though these are usually expressed in general terms, such as the number of rooms or floor space required per household member, there is still considerable scope for variation in the specification of required standards, and these can be a source of quite large differences in the estimates of total housing need and its cost. For example, existing standards of accommodation may be adopted as a benchmark, but these will be a poor guide to actual needs if they simply reflect adjustments to the available stock. Obviously, when projections are being made over very long periods it should be recognised that attitudes concerning acceptable standards are likely to change in the future. On the subject of specifying standards, Needleman has pointed out the dangers inherent in a system where the planners who set standards are also responsible for their attainment. This, he argues, may well lead to excessive caution in defining standards.[15]

When the issues concerning standards have been resolved, the estimates of the stock of housing required at different points during the forecast period may be compared with the existing stock to determine the number of additional dwellings needed. As well as the dwellings required for additional households, provision will need to be made for the replacement of existing dwellings that are either unsuitable or likely to become so through age and obsolescence, or are likely to be demolished during the period. Indeed, the high average age of British housing and the long duration of need forecast periods can mean that replacement needs are quantitatively more important than those for new households. Stone (1970) estimated that about seven million additional dwellings would be required to supplement the existing stock in the forty-year period between 1964 and 2004, but that replacement demand could add another four to twelve millions to this total, depending upon the type of replacement policy adopted.

Finally, a margin of vacant dwellings will need to be added to the stock requirements to allow for household mobility between dwellings and areas, and also to satisfy the desire for second homes. The actual number of dwellings required to facilitate movement will depend upon the extent of movement: in the past a vacancy rate of around 1 per cent has permitted 6 per cent of the population to move each year in Britain, whereas a 2 per cent vacancy rate has been sufficient to allow 20 per cent of the US population to move each year. The number of dwellings required for second homes will tend to increase as higher incomes, and possibly shorter working time, lead to greater expenditure on leisure activities. Overall, Needleman (1961) estimated that a margin of about 4 per cent of the stock should, by 1980, be sufficient to satisfy requirements for vacant dwellings arising from the desire for movement and second homes.

CHAPTER FIVE

The Supply of Housing

The capital stock adjustment model outlined in Chapter Three shows how changes in the demand for housing lead to changes in the rate of construction of new dwellings. The precise form of this relationship, and indeed the general responsiveness of the supply of housing services to the various demands for them, will depend upon the nature of the construction industry. In this chapter an analysis of this industry is presented. Its aim is to identify those features of the industry which are important in determining the way supply-side factors influence market performance rather than to provide a detailed description of the industry. However, some appreciation of the industry's organisation and structure is a necessary prerequisite for understanding its performance, and so this is dealt with in the course of the next section. This is followed by an analysis of the cost conditions found in the industry which includes a discussion of the choice of building techniques and forms.

The Construction Process

So far it has been a convenient simplification to speak of the construction industry as if there are a set of reasonably homogeneous firms concerned with the production of housing. But a more detailed analysis reveals that this is clearly not the case. Bowley, for example, refers to the industry as 'an enormous mosaic in which different types of pieces represent different services, firms, products, markets, owners with no inherent modular element to ensure effective fit'.[1] However, within this 'mosaic' Stone (1970) is able to identify three main sectors: one responsible for planning, design and related work; another comprising firms engaged in the production of building materials; and a third concerned with the actual building, or assembly process. The supply of housing – which, it should be noted, is by no means the sole output of this industry[2] – involves a combination of the complex set of activities carried out both within and between these sectors. A typical arrangement of these activities is shown in Figure 5.1.

The construction process begins with demand from a client. Increasingly, the client will tend to be an organisation which either lets dwellings to tenants (for example, a Local Authority, a housing

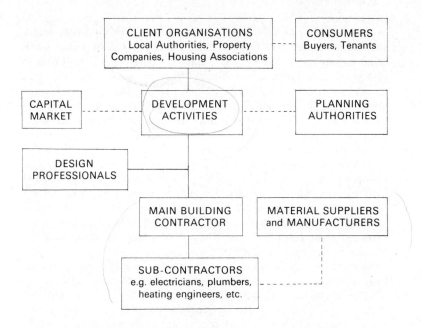

Figure 5.1   The development process

association or a private property company) or sells them to house buyers, rather than an individual consumer. Thus the initiator of the building process is usually part of the supply side of the industry. Moreover, in many cases, building takes place in anticipation of finding buyers or renters when the dwellings are completed, and for this reason it is often referred to as speculative building. It is, of course, not unusual to find an industry in which the need for large-scale investment before production can proceed means that decisions to produce a good are made in anticipation of future sales rather than in response to existing demands. However, in the construction industry, the lack of co-ordination resulting from the existence of a large number of small firms, the length of the construction period and the frequency of short-term changes in demand, all combine to make speculative building a source of considerable instability (see Chapter Three).

However, before building work can even start various preliminary tasks need to be carried out. These have been referred to in Figure 5.1 as 'development activities'. They include, for example, the need to obtain credit to cover the costs of the project and the receipt of planning consent from the relevant planning authority. Credit facilities are necessary because the long gestation period in this industry means that there is a considerable lapse of time between the start of work and the eventual sale of the product. Start-to-completion times of up to two years are commonplace. During this period bridging finance is usually necessary to cover the costs incurred. The price and availability of credit will therefore play an important part in determining supply-side behaviour just as it does in determining the demand for housing. The second preliminary task involves obtaining planning permission. This is necessary for practically all building work. In the case of small developments involving a few houses and no major changes of land use, this is unlikely to be a difficult or protracted business. On the other hand, the receipt of planning permission for a large-scale development, which has marked implications for other land users, will only follow a lengthy and detailed scrutiny of the project by the planning authorities. Sometimes a formal planning inquiry under an Inspector appointed by the Department of the Environment may be necessary. Obviously these deliberations take time and often lead to delays in the development process. In fact, some commentators have argued that the failure of LAs to release sufficient land for building purposes has been a major contributory factor towards the house price inflation of recent years. However, it should be borne in mind that this criticism emphasises only the costs of planning whereas a full evaluation would require its benefits to be considered as well.[3]

After the initial assembly of loan finance and the receipt of planning approval, the services of the first of Stone's three main sectors are engaged; that is, the planning and design professionals. These include the architects, surveyors, engineers and others concerned with the details of the built form. Traditionally, these services have been carried out prior to, and separate from, the building stage. This fact has attracted the criticism of Bowley (1966), who claims that the divorce of design and production, together with a lack of competition at the design stage, have been major obstacles to technical progress and innovation within the industry. The separation of design and production has, she argues, led to a lack of awareness on the part of designers about developments in building technology. Moreover, the absence of any competitive pressure among them has removed any incentive to innovate with the result that they have tended to favour traditional designs instead of innovatory building forms which would allow new construction techniques to be employed. In recent years, however, there has been a trend towards involving builders in the design stage. Sometimes this is achieved through negotiations between the developer and the builder; in other cases, builders actually offer 'package deals' incorporating design services.[4]

When detailed design plans have been drawn up they are passed to the next sector of the industry which is responsible for the actual building work. This is usually done through the appointment of a main building contractor. Various methods for selecting a main contractor are used, ranging from the competitive bidding of an open tender to selective or serial tendering arrangements.[5] Once appointed, the main contractor will, in turn, subcontract various parts of the work to specialist firms. The extent of this subcontracting is indicated by the number of subdivisions within the construction industry reported in the 1974 Census of Production. This lists twenty separate groupings including general builders (38 872 undertakings), plumbers (7 924), painters (14 273) carpenters (6 085), roofers (1 966), plasterers (3 237), electrical contractors (6 318) and plant hirers (2 009). In total, the census identifies nearly 28 000 subcontractors: this represents 30 per cent of undertakings which Balchin and Kieve (1977) suggest account for about 40 per cent of the industry's gross output. Now while it is not unusual for an industry to comprise a number of separate firms working on different stages of the production process, the extent of subcontracting within the building industry itself does perhaps require some explanation.

A number of reasons can be put forward to explain the growth of subcontracting. First, there is the uncertainty of workload that faces firms in an industry that is subject to large fluctuations in the demand for new building. This encourages firms to minimise their fixed cost commitments as these will still be incurred in periods of slack demand when capacity is under-utilised. In consequence, main contractors try to convert fixed costs into variable costs wherever possible. One way in which this may be achieved is by hiring capital equipment instead of buying it. Another is by employing subcontracted labour services on a job-to-job basis and thereby avoiding the problems of under-employed labour and/or the redundancy and other severance payments which would be incurred with a permanent labour force in times of fluctuating demand. For their part, small specialist subcontracting firms often survive the fluctuations in demand from the new building industry by concentrating on the more stable repair and maintenance side of the business. There is also sometimes scope for firms to obtain work in the commercial, industrial or civil engineering construction sectors when housing demand falls. But the consequences of fluctuating demand cannot be avoided completely, and both unemployment rates and the birth/mortality rates of firms in construction are substantially higher than in most other industries.[6]

A second reason for the division of work between different firms is that the nature of much building work is still craft based and labour-intensive. Consequently there is little scope for combining the work of the carpenter and the plumber, or the bricklayer and the electrician; nor is there much opportunity for substituting capital for labour and thereby reaping economies of scale within particular trades. Hence there is little to be gained at the production stage through the amalgamation of firms, either between or within trades. None the less, it might be thought that there could be potential organisational economies of scale to be gained by combining various trades within a single firm, but in practice this is unlikely to be the case. To appreciate why this is so, it is necessary to explain the way in which different labour inputs are combined in the construction process; in particular, the existence of widely varying labour-output ratios. Table 5.1 shows the estimated number of man-days required per £1 000 contract for some of the main building trades.

TABLE 5.1
*Building labour inputs for selected trades**

	Man-days per £1000 contract at 1970 prices	
	House-building	Repair and maintenance
Carpenters	7.7	15.0
Bricklayers	10.0	5.0
Painters	5.4	12.0
Electricians	1.6	7.0
Plumbers	2.6	6.0
Heating and ventilating	0.3	4.0
General labourers	17.0	24.0

* Building Research Establishment estimated coefficients.
Source: *Construction in the Early 1980s*, Building and Civil Engineering EDC (HMSO, 1976).

Clearly there are substantial variations in the amounts of different types of labour time required. Moreover, most specialised services represent only a small proportion of the total workload and are very often restricted to a particular stage of the building timetable. Thus bricklayers are required for different periods of time and at different stages to carpenters, painters for different periods and at different stages to plasterers, and so on. The result of these complicated input mixes is that it would be very difficult for a single firm that employed all the necessary specialists to arrange a workload that would ensure their full employment at all times. This is likely to be achieved rather more easily in a firm employing a single type of specialist because it will be able to organise its work over a range of contractors and a large number of projects.

Most of the trades involved in the building process are, in essence, assembling on the site materials that have been produced elsewhere. The provision of materials and the conditions under which they are supplied are therefore of considerable importance to the performance of the building industry. This is the province of the material and components manufacturing sector. It includes brick, cement, steel, plastic, wood products and many other industries. The scale of output in these industries — which is often increased because they supply other markets besides the construction sector — is sufficiently great for economies of scale to have led to a degree of concentration that is far higher than in other areas of the construction industry. Indeed, as is shown in the next section, many of the cost-reducing technical advances developed within the construction industry have involved substituting factory processes for on-site work.

This concludes a brief account of the construction process. It has been designed to show the network of interrelationships that make up the construction industry. In the case of some of the largest firms vertical integration has proceeded to the point where many functions are performed within the same firm, but in most cases there is a large amount of devolution and subcontracting. This introduces considerable problems of coordination and, as far as supply responses are concerned, can be a source of delay and instability. But this pattern of industrial organisation has not developed through chance. It has been argued above that there are reasons for subcontracting by specialism among building trades. In the next section this question is pursued further in an attempt to assess the efficiency of the building industry.

Cost Conditions

The conventional way of assessing the economic efficiency of a firm or industry is to examine its costs per unit of output. Thus probably the most widely used procedure is to relate unit costs to the level or scale of output to determine the optimum level of output for a given plant or firm or, in the longer term, the optimum plant or firm size. But other considerations may also be relevant. For example, technological developments may offer a choice of techniques; in building, these relate to both the methods of construction and the type of building form. Accordingly, this section will look at the relative costs of industrialised building methods compared with traditional techniques, and the choice between high-rise and low-rise building, as well as more general cost-output relationships.

Costs and the Level of Output

Empirical evidence on the relationship between unit costs and output should help us to answer two key questions. The first of these relates to short-run cost conditions, that is, to what extent will unit costs vary as a result of the unintended changes in the levels of output following the fluctuations in demand to which this industry is particularly susceptible? And second, does the evidence on long-run costs suggest that the existing size distribution of firms is an efficient one?

On the question of short-run costs, Hillebrandt (1974) has examined the likely effect upon unit costs of deviations in output from the optimum level for the typical building firm.[7] She identifies two main variable cost items: materials used on the site — which account for around one-half of average total costs at the optimum level, and site labour unit costs — which represent about one-third of average total costs. Both of these can be expected to be constant for much of the output range although some increases may be experienced if very large deviations from the optimum take place when, for example, cost savings obtainable from material bulk-buying arrangements are lost, or the labour force is under-utilised. Overall, however, the constancy of these costs and the fact that they represent over 80 per cent of total costs compared with the less than 10 per cent accounted for by fixed costs, means that the short-run average cost curve of the typical construction firm is horizontal in the region of its optimum output. Clearly this makes it easier for it to endure fluctuations in demand than would be the case if average costs rose steeply from their minimum point.

Long-run cost conditions indicate the relative efficiency of different scales of production; that is, the unit costs that a firm can achieve at different levels of output when it is free to vary all its factor inputs. It has already been argued in the previous section that there are limited opportunities for obtaining economies of scale in the traditional building process and this view is certainly consistent with the preponderance of small firms, as shown in Table 5.2.

The table shows that approximately 90 per cent of firms employ twenty-five persons or less. It is, however, the heterogeneity of the industry's output that is crucial in explaining the observed size distribution of firms. For example, Hillebrandt (1971) in a study of the construction industry carried out for the Bolton Committee of Inquiry on Small Firms estimated that output per head was

TABLE 5.2

The construction industry: analysis of undertakings by size, 1974

Size group: numbers employed

	1–19	20–49	50–99	100–199	200–499	500–999	1000–2499	2500–4999	over 5000	Total
Number of Undertakings	84 184	6 392	1 882	934	541	218	116	24	14	94 305
% of total Undertakings	89.3	6.8	2.0	1.0	0.6	0.2	0.1	0.03	0.01	100
Net output (£000s)	1 096 482	695 424	503 821	524 072	673 405	599 093	666 574	328 333	536 607	5 623 811
% of total net output	19.5	12.4	9.0	9.0	12.0	10.7	11.9	5.8	9.5	100

approximately one-third higher in large firms[8] — a result which, by itself, could be expected to lead to a greater concentration of output in the more efficient large firm sector. However, the differential varied substantially between different types of work. In housing maintenance and repair work, for example, it was at most equal to 5 per cent. And it is significant that 70 per cent of this work was carried out by small firms.[9] On the other hand, small firms accounted for less than 30 per cent of new housing work where, for many projects, their labour productivity is substantially below that of the larger firms.

Thus, although statistics on the degree of output concentration show that there has been some decline in the share of work carried out by small firms in recent years,[10] the survival of an extensive small-firm sector certainly suggests that for many of the traditional building activities economies of scale do not exist. But what is the scope for replacing traditional processes by other methods which do yield economies of scale? In many industries this has been achieved by the substitution of capital for labour; in building this process is usually associated with industrialised or systems building methods.

Industrialised Building

The term 'industrialised' or 'systems' building is usually used to refer to those methods of construction which substitute factory manufacture of standard prefabricated units and components for traditional labour-intensive *in situ* site work. (Sometimes the term is used more generally to refer to methods of work organisation as well, but this section concentrates on the more narrow definition.) By this transfer of work, Seeley (1974) estimates that site labour requirements can be reduced from approximately 1 800 man-hours per dwelling using traditional methods to 700–1 300 hours using industrialised techniques. Moreover, if the production of such standard components as prefabricated windows, doors and staircases, precast concrete, steel structures and plastics, etc., is carried out in a factory serving many different projects and sites, the scale of output can be sufficiently large and stable to merit the installation of labour-saving capital equipment. Few lone projects are large enough to make this worthwhile. Thus given the limited opportunities for mechanising traditional methods on-site, industrialised building seeks to replace them by more capital-intensive off-site work.

However, the application of industrialised methods has been far less widespread than might have been expected ten years ago. An indication of their decline in popularity is provided by statistics on the percentage of LA dwellings built by industrialised methods. Following the peak year of 1970 when over 40 per cent of dwellings were built using these methods, the percentage has subsequently fallen annually until by 1976 they accounted for less than 20 per cent of dwellings.[11] The reason why industrialised building methods have failed to be adopted more widely is simply that they have produced few overall cost savings. A number of factors have led to this state of affairs. A major one is that those building forms for which industrialised methods were particularly suited − especially high-rise flats − have been used only infrequently since the late 1960s (see the next section). On the other hand, results with other building forms have been disappointing. One reason for this is the high transport cost of moving prefabricated units from the factory to the building site. Even in an unassembled form many building components tend to be large, bulky and heavy, but of low value in relation to their size. This results in a high transport cost-to-value ratio. A second factor is the need for extremely strict, and therefore expensive, quality control in the factory manufacturing process. The elimination of site craft labour means that there is less opportunity for making marginal adjustments to fittings on the site with the result that the degree of precision in dimensioning needs to be far higher than is required for most traditional materials. Finally, the relative costs of various building factor inputs means that there is less scope for making savings through this type of industrialisation in Britain than there is in many other countries. For example, savings in site labour time are savings in skilled time that are partly offset by increases in non-skilled, factory labour time. In many countries the differential between skilled site and unskilled factory wage rates is large enough to yield substantial cost savings, but in Britain this is not the case. Again, the traditional British building material, the brick, is not suited to industrialised methods. But it is cheap to produce compared with the traditional materials used in many other countries and therefore there is less reason to replace it with more expensive materials better suited to industrialised methods.

For all these reasons, industrialised processes have failed to reduce costs of production sufficiently to justify large-scale investment in industrialised plant and machinery. Only in the case of large-scale high-rise developments have building costs been reduced significantly below the levels obtainable through traditional methods. Thus by 1971 tender prices for LA flats in buildings of five or more storeys were about 18 per cent cheaper if industrialised methods were involved.[12] Yet after tremendous initial popularity these building forms have faded from fashion. Why has this happened?

High-rise versus Low-rise Building

The major advantage claimed for high-rise building is, of course, that it is less expensive in terms of land requirements. The pressures of urban development have resulted in both a shortage of inner-city building land enjoying the necessary locational attributes and, at the periphery of the city, the encroachment of building on agricultural land and other green space. By building upwards less land per dwelling is needed and these pressures are eased somewhat. However, unless the land constraint is allowed to dominate all others, what matters is the total cost of building not just its land cost. Land designated for building should be valued in terms of its opportunity cost alongside all the other factor inputs. (Shadow prices can be used to reflect the value of land if it is felt that market prices underestimate its value; this might be considered appropriate given the irreversible nature of many decisions involving building on undeveloped land.) The way in which both land and relative building costs will determine the optimal building height is demonstrated in Figure 5.2.

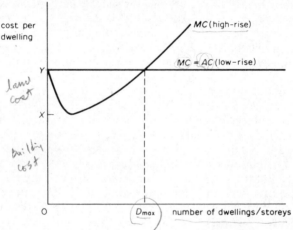

Figure 5.2   Comparative costs of high-rise and low-rise building

In the example shown in Figure 5.2, we have assumed that dwellings can be built either in single storeys, in which case a separate plot of land is required for each dwelling, or in multiple storeys on a single plot of land. Thus the horizontal axis measures the number of dwellings in the case of a single-storey development, whereas in the case of a multi-storey project it shows the number of dwellings *and* the number of storeys. Now the cost per dwelling in a single-storey development is equal to the building cost (OX) plus the cost of land (XY). This remains constant however many dwellings are built because each one simply duplicates those built earlier: hence the average cost is the same as the marginal cost. (For purposes of illustration any economies of scale that may exist have been ignored. This will not affect the general principles of this example as these economies are equally likely to be present in both high- and low-rise developments.) The cost per dwelling in a high-rise development will fall initially as the second and subsequent dwellings do not incur any additional land costs. But as the height of construction rises so the level of building costs increases. Reasons for these higher costs include the additional labour and material handling expenses incurred in working above ground level, the need for the installation of lifts and rubbish disposal systems, more intricate and lengthy plumbing and heating arrangements, etc.[13] This leads to a marginal cost schedule of the form depicted in the diagram: at first it declines but then it rises until it eventually moves above the schedule for single-storey dwellings. The point of intersection of the two schedules indicates the maximum number of storeys that can be built before the additional building costs incurred on a high-rise dwelling become greater than the land cost of a comparable single-storey dwelling.

It is when a general appraisal of the above form is carried out that the high-rise building alternative appears less attractive. For example, estimates produced by the National Institute for Economic and Social Research[14] show the magnitude of the substantial increases in building costs incurred on a standard London flat of 680 sq. ft as the building height rises. Compared with a dwelling in a one- or two-storey building, one in a five-storey building would be 17 per cent more expensive to build, in a ten-storey building it would be 35 per cent more costly, and in a fifteen-storey block it would be 44 per cent more expensive. Outside London the differentials were even larger. In another study, Needleman calculated the price of land per acre necessary to offset the additional costs of building high. Although his figures are now out of date, his conclusion that 'land has to be very expensive before there is any saving in building even three-storey flats instead of two-storey houses'[15] still remains true for most sites. Indeed, in some cases, even the savings in land realised through high-rise development have been negligible because the provision of surrounding green space and other public facilities has had to be more extensive than that provided for households living in low-rise accommodation.

But probably the main factor leading to the decline in high-rise building for residential purposes has not been an economic one at all. Rather it has been the growing body of evidence (and community pressure associated with it) pointing out the deleterious effect on many households of high-rise living conditions. This is especially true of families with children, who require easy access to visible play areas – a facility which living fifteen floors above the ground clearly does not provide. As a result of these considerations, planning preferences have shifted towards low- and medium-rise housing, which, incidentally, it has been found can achieve the same densities as high-rise schemes if planned skilfully.

PART THREE

Aspects of Policy

CHAPTER SIX

Rent Control

Rent control is frequently cited by writers of elementary economics textbooks as an example of a price control policy which, by restricting price below its equilibrium level, can be expected to result in an unsatisfied excess demand for housing and a reduction in its supply.[1] At a more polemical level, there are a number of tracts which relate these general theoretical predictions to various empirical indicators of housing shortage and other alleged deleterious effects of rent control. Literature of this type usually contains a recommendation for a return to some form of unrestricted free market in rented housing.[2] At the other end of the spectrum, a very different approach has been adopted by writers on social administration. For the most part, they have been extremely wary about the generality of economic theorising and have preferred to proceed by employing detailed empirical analyses of housing policy and market behaviour.[3] Thus the person interested in examining the impact of rent control is likely to encounter something of a gap in the approach adopted towards the subject: one group of writers employing a formal theoretical framework but, at best, only partial empirical data, and at the other extreme, a group of writers collecting a great deal of empirical evidence but in many cases rejecting *a priori* (and therefore not testing adequately) certain general theoretical expectations about the way the market functions.[4] In this chapter we shall attempt to bridge this gap by discussing both the general theoretical expectations of rent control and the empirical evidence of its effects. In so doing, we shall draw on the work of both schools of thought, as well as using certain pieces of empirical data that have recently become available.

In the first section of the chapter, we have considered some of the major theoretical aspects of rent control policy. In particular, we have used the housing capital stock adjustment model outlined in Chapter Two to consider the impact that rent control is likely to have on market price and output. Then, before moving on to consider whether the empirical evidence supports the various hypotheses suggested by the model, we have presented a brief review of the form in which rent control has been applied in Britain over the last sixty years. This is necessary because the policy has been far from uniform and, accordingly, expectations about its effects will vary. In the next section we present the bulk of the empirical evidence. The final section is devoted to a rather more detailed examination of the particular form of rent control, rent *regulation*, that has been in force in Britain since 1965.

The Housing Market and Rent Control: Theoretical Considerations

We may begin by defining rent control as a policy designed to protect tenants from the high market rents which otherwise would result from a shortage in the supply of rented housing. Although the policy may take many forms, it usually involves specifying the maximum rent that a landlord may charge a tenant for a dwelling – a rent that is below the short-run market level. In addition, to be effective, the policy also requires that a tenant should be guaranteed a minimum standard of accommodation and the right to continue to occupy a dwelling at the designated rent. For this reason, rent control has usually been accompanied by measures specifying minimum standards and offering security of tenure. Thus the price and terms of the transaction between the landlord and tenant are subject to specific statutory control. Obviously this has a number of consequences.

To start with the policy clearly involves a redistribution of income from landlords to tenants. By depressing rents below their free market level, control gives the tenant a subsidy equal to the difference between the controlled and the market rent. However, unlike most other subsidy schemes where the government decides that a particular group merits assistance, in this case the government does not meet the cost of the subsidy itself, but requires it to be met by the private landlord. Questions that are likely to arise in this context are: is the form of redistribution that takes place consistent with society's general objectives concerning the distribution of income? And, if it is, is rent control an efficient method for achieving the prescribed objective?

Regarding the first question, it may be that society's welfare function ranks the interests of tenants (qua tenants) more highly than those of landlords (for some people, landlords' interests figure hardly, if at all, in their utility functions!), but the most widely-accepted criterion for ranking is likely to be on the basis of relative income levels. This being the case, to assess the policy we need to know about the relative income levels of the two groups. This is an empirical question to which we shall return in the third section of the chapter.

The second question relates to the efficiency of rent control as an instrument for redistributing income. This raises the general issue of the relative merits of policies providing assistance through income-in-kind, or price subsidisation, and those providing it through general income supplementation. This issue is considered in the context of Local Authority housing in Chapter Eight. More specifically, however, even if a policy which affects relative prices is accepted, there remain a number of particular criticisms which are often levelled against rent control. Notable among these are: (1) that by reducing the profitability of rented housing it leads to a reduction in the supply of such housing, (2) the reduction in profitability also leads to a neglect of the existing stock of housing and a resultant deterioration in its quality, (3) it leads to underoccupation and (4) it leads to a reduction in household mobility. Let us examine the theoretical arguments on which each of these assertions is based, starting with the claim about a reduction in supply.

Rent Control and the Supply of Housing

The housing market may, as we saw in Chapter Three, be represented in terms of a capital stock adjustment model. Accordingly Figure 6.1 reproduces the main features of Figure 3.1, except that on this occasion it refers solely to private rented housing.

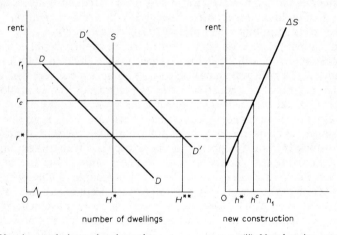

(i) Housing stock demand and supply   (ii) New housing supply

Figure 6.1   Housing stock adjustment and rent control

Suppose that the market for rented housing is initially in long-run equilibrium at a rent level of r^*. At this rent the housing stock is equal to $0H^*$, and the supply of new dwellings per year, $0h^*$, is just sufficient to offset obsolescence and maintain a constant stock size. Now further suppose that there is a sudden increase in the demand for rented accommodation. Historically this has often occurred when there has been large-scale in-migration to certain areas over a short period of time, especially in wartime. The increase in demand would result in the short-run rent of the fixed stock of dwellings being bid up to r_1. Now as r_1 is above the long-run equilibrium level of r^*, there will be an incentive for landlords to add to the stock of dwellings. Hence, in time it may be expected that the size of the stock will increase – by annual increments – until the original rent level, r^*, is re-established at the new stock of $0H^{**}$ (assuming constant long-run costs). However, this adjustment process may take many years to reach completion, especially if constraints on housebuilding exist because of special circumstances, such as wartime shortages of materials for domestic consumption. In consequence, the government may feel that the initial rise in rents is unacceptable and it may, therefore, specify a maximum controlled rent of r_c. Now it should be noted that $r^* < r_c < r_1$, that is, the controlled rent is above the long-run equilibrium rent but below the short-run market level. If this is a feature of the controlled rent, it will affect the *rate* at which adjustment to a new equilibrium takes place, but it will not affect the final long-run outcome. This point is worth stressing for it is frequently neglected in discussions about rent control. Specifically, in terms of Figure 6.1, the first year's addition to the stock will be $0h^c$ instead of $0h_1$, and in each subsequent year the annual increment will be similarly smaller. But a stock of $0H^{**}$ will be achieved eventually. Thus, in such cases, shortages of housing can be said to arise because of rent control in so far as the rate of new construction is lower than it otherwise would be, but it should not lead to lasting shortages.

On the other hand, if controlled rents are, as it is frequently claimed, set below the long-run equilibrium level, then a reduction in the stock of rented property can be expected. Furthermore, under these conditions, there is no positive lower limit to the size of the stock. For unlike the example discussed in Chapter Three (where a reduction in the size of the stock, following a decrease in demand and price, leads eventually to a price rise and the re-establishment of the long-run equilibrium price) when the controlled rent is prevented from rising and kept permanently below r^*, the decline in the stock will continue each year because rent levels will not be sufficiently high to induce even replacement building. Moreover, the rate of decline may be accelerated above the rate of physical obsolescence if landlords are able to obtain higher returns by transferring their property to alternative uses. A frequently cited example of this strategy is the sale of erstwhile rented property for owner-occupation – in this way the landlord's asset is capitalised in a market where price controls do not exist.

On the other hand, however, even if controlled rents are set below the long-run equilibrium level, there may well be certain institutional constraints which slow down the rate of decline. For example, rent-controlling legislation usually provides the tenant with some form of security of tenure which limits the landlord's ability to dispose of his property or convert it to alternative uses.[5] However, while this constraint may reduce the rate at which the stock of rented dwellings declines, it is often claimed that it has produced another undesirable side effect: that is, a landlord receiving an inadequate rate of return from his property – and unable to dispose of it at an acceptable price – will have little incentive to undertake any further investment in it. The result will be a neglect of maintenance and repair expenditure, and a deterioration in the quality of the stock.

The Quality of Rented Housing

Moorhouse (1972) and Frankena (1975) have developed formal models to show how reducing maintenance and repair expenditure will be the optimal response for the profit-maximising landlord faced with rent control. In their work they both make use of the concept of housing as a vector of attributes. As we showed in Chapter One, it is these attributes which yield units of housing services – units which will vary both quantitatively and qualitatively. Thus the rent (r) a landlord receives for a dwelling may be expressed as the sum of the average price per unit of services (p) multiplied by the number of units supplied (q), that is $r = p.q$. Rent control of the conventional type will be in the form of an overall revenue per dwelling constraint which specifies a maximum rent, r_c. If $r_c < r^*$ then the price per unit of services he receives will be depressed below its equilibrium level, and it is this price together with the cost per unit of services that will determine the landlord's rate of profit. However, this price is not controlled directly. Therefore, the landlord may be expected to respond by raising p, although he cannot do so while q remains constant because this would cause him to exceed the overall revenue constraint r_c placed on his dwelling. But he can do so by reducing q and simultaneously increasing p. Thus if we assume that his unit costs are either constant or rise more slowly than p as he reduces output, by a reduction in maintenance and repair expenditure he can reduce q, raise p and protect his rate of return.

This response is represented diagrammatically in Figure 6.2. The initial stock equilibrium condition is similar to that shown in Figure 6.1 except that now the axes indicate the units of housing *services* and their price per unit. If a controlled rent per dwelling of r_c is set below r^*, then the price per unit of q falls to p_1. The landlord may be

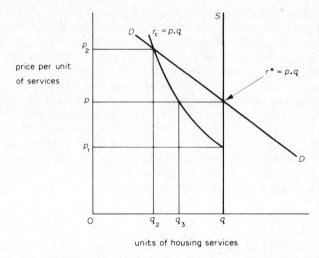

Figure 6.2   Rent control and housing quality adjustments

expected to respond by reducing the number of units of housing service offered – from a given number of dwellings – and raising their price per unit. The revenue constraint represented by rent control simply ensures that the price–quantity combination stays on, or below, the rectangular hyperbole traced by r_c. If the quantity of housing services falls to q_2, an equilibrium will be established between the demand and supply of housing services and there will be no tendency for any further decline to take place. It may be, however, that public health legislation on housing minimum standards prevents a fall to q_2. This will not necessarily prevent the landlord from obtaining his required price per unit of services (for example, this could be obtained at any quantity below q_3) but it will mean that an excess demand for rent-controlled housing will exist with the associated likelihood of black market practices emerging (for example, key money, payments for fixtures and fittings).

Under-occupation and Household Mobility

In addition to its alleged impact on the quantity and quality of rented housing, it is frequently asserted that rent control encourages the 'overconsumption' of housing and has led to a reduction in household mobility. The first claim is a straightforward application of consumer demand theory which predicts that a reduction in the price of a commodity will lead to a greater quantity being demanded. Thus the control of rents below the market level, it is argued, leads to greater consumption of housing space than would occur in an unregulated market and therefore, by this standard, there is overconsumption: or, as it is more frequently expressed, underoccupation. The second claim concerning household mobility is associated with a particular form of rent-control policy that has been operated in Britain whereby only existing tenancies are controlled (see next section for a more detailed account). In such circumstances a tenant who quits a controlled property is not likely to be able to find alternative housing at a rent similar to his previous controlled level. Hence there is a disincentive for him to move. This is seen as a particularly undesirable side-effect of control when the labour market requires mobility.

To summarise the discussion of this section, we may note that the housing market is characterised by extreme stock supply inelasticity which, in the face of periodic increases in demand, will lead to high short-run rents. During the stock adjustment process, which may take several years, substantial monopoly profits may be expected to accrue to the owners of existing rental housing. Rent control provides one means of protecting tenants from these abnormally high short-run rents but it may be expected to have several other consequences. Notably, it may influence the supply of housing, either by slowing the rate of stock adjustment or, more seriously, by encouraging a reduction in the size of the stock. Furthermore, it may lead to under-investment in maintenance and repair work and a consequent deterioration in the quality of the existing stock. Finally, two subsidiary criticisms of rent control are often cited: that it reduces household mobility and, through unwarranted price subsidisation, causes suboptimal consumption patterns.

Some empirical analysis should enable us to test these hypotheses. However, as we shall see, there have been a number of versions of rent control applied in Britain, each of which may be expected to have had rather different results. Clearly, therefore, before we can evaluate the policy we need to be aware of its different forms. Consequently, the next section provides a brief account of some of the main features of successive policies over the period 1915–75.

Rent-Control Policies

Rent control was first introduced in Britain in 1915 as one of a number of price controls designed to protect consumers from the inflationary conditions that were expected to arise because of wartime shortages. The Act which introduced the policy froze the majority of rents at their immediate pre-war levels or at the rent at which they were first let. Initially, the control was viewed as an *ad hoc* emergency measure that could be dispensed with at the end of the war when normal conditions were re-established. However, when the war finished, the extent of the housing shortage, the supply problems of the construction industry and a political climate committed to providing 'homes fit for heroes' all combined to make it an unfavourable time to decontrol rents. Consequently, further Acts were passed in 1919 and 1920 which extended the period of control and the scope of the earlier Act. At the time, the policy was still referred to as a temporary measure, but in fact this marked the beginning of an era of peacetime intervention in the pricing decisions of the private rented market for housing that has continued to the present day.

The main Acts covering rent-control policy over the period 1915–75 are listed, together with their major provisions, in Table 6.1. Without going too far into the intricacies of this formidable list of legislation it is nevertheless possible to identify certain key features of the policy as it has been applied at various times.[6] First, its most straightforward and rigid application is represented by *full control*. Under this restriction all designated property is subject to a maximum controlled rent which is usually related to a level it has reached at some specified date in the past. This policy was implemented at the beginning of each war and, in the case of the second war, retained for a considerable period afterwards.

At other times, policies of full control have been gradually replaced by a system of decontrol which attempts to minimise the impact of rent increases on existing tenants. These are often referred to as systems of *gradual or creeping decontrol*. Under this policy, a property remains controlled until the existing tenancy ends; control is, therefore, transferred from the property to the tenant and ends when he moves. A third phase of policy has occurred when it has been felt that the housing demand and supply conditions are sufficiently in balance to allow a full-scale cessation of control without a rapid rise in rents ensuing. The introduction of decontrol, without the prerequisite of the ending of an existing tenancy, is usually referred to as *block decontrol*. Finally, the most recent phase of rent-control policy was implemented in 1965 with the introduction of rent *regulation*. Through this policy a system of 'fair rents' was applied to most of the housing stock decontrolled under the 1957 Act. Regulation is more flexible than any of the earlier policies we have described because it specifies the fair rent of each individual dwelling in relation to its specific characteristics. Moreover, it provides for periodic rent reviews and generally aims to establish greater equity between landlords and tenants than previous policies. (We shall return to this policy for a more detailed consideration in the last section.)

TABLE 6.1
UK rent-controlling legislation 1915–75

1915	Full rent control introduced. Most rents restricted to immediate pre-war level.
1919	Scope of control extended to include more expensive houses and houses built since the first Act. General increases in rent of up to 40 per cent above 1914 level permitted to cover increased costs. Rents of houses built for rent after 1919 not controlled.
1923	Gradual or 'creeping' decontrol introduced.
1933	Full control reintroduced for lower-valued property; creeping decontrol retained for middle-valued property and block decontrol introduced for higher-valued property.
1937	Ridley Committee Report recommends (i) block decontrol for middle-income housing, and (ii) adoption of geographical 'overcrowding indices' as a basis for further decontrol.
1938	First Ridley recommendation implemented.
1939	Outbreak of Second World War; general full control reintroduced.
1954	Rent increases of twice the 'statutory deduction' permitted to cover repairs expenditure. No general relaxation on rent control.
1957	Block decontrol of all higher-valued property introduced (i.e. rateable value $> £40$ in London and $> £30$ elsewhere) and creeping decontrol of all other property.
1965	Rent 'regulation' on the basis of 'fair rents' introduced for decontrolled property.
1974	Fair rent policy and security of tenure provisions extended to include 'furnished' accommodation.

As Table 6.1 indicates, for much of the period under consideration each of these aspects of the policy has been applied to different sectors of the market at the same time. For example, the 1933 Act imposed full control on all lower-valued property, creeping decontrol for middle-valued property and released higher-valued property (via block decontrol) from all control. Again, the controversial 1957 Act – which was in many ways modelled on the 1933 Act –

introduced creeping decontrol for lower-valued property while more highly-valued property was decontrolled en bloc. Moreover, the varied application of the policy was likely to have been extended beyond rateable value categories if the Second World War had not intervened, for in 1937, the Ridley Committee had recommended a more flexible approach to rent control, an approach to be based on local conditions through the use of overcrowding indices, and, as we shall see, this was in some respects a precursor of the 1965 Act.

This concludes our brief description of the form that rent-control policy has taken. However, before moving on to examine whether the empirical data associated with each of these policy periods support the theoretical hypotheses outlined in the previous section, one other important aspect of the policy as it was applied between 1915 and 1965 needs to be mentioned. This concerns the treatment of new construction, specifically the fact that under the policies operated between 1923–39 and 1954–65 new property built for renting was excluded from rent-control provisions. This is obviously an important factor to be taken into account when assessing the effect of rent control on the supply of new housing.

Rent Control: Empirical Evidence

To what extent have the policies described in the last section produced the results mentioned earlier? Specifically, have rents been kept below long-run equilibrium levels? If so, how has this affected the supply and quality of rental housing? Moreover, does the evidence support the view that rent control has 'distorted' housing consumption patterns? And, finally, what of the equity of rent control: does it redistribute income from the better to the less well-off, or not? In this section we shall attempt to provide some answers to these questions.

Rent Levels

Evidence about controlled rent levels in the early part of the period is difficult to obtain but it is likely that in the ten years 1923–33 they were not much, if at all, below current market levels. Nevitt argues that the 15 to 40 per cent rent increases permitted by the 1923 Act enabled investors to get a 'competitive return on their capital' during a period when most incomes and prices were actually falling (the retail price index fell by nearly 20 per cent over the same period).[7] For the remainder of the inter-war period, however, prices began to rise again, and it is likely that the investment return offered by controlled rents was less than could have been obtained elsewhere. Phelps Brown and

Wiseman (1964) maintain that by 1939 controlled rents were 20 to 30 per cent below the uncontrolled level for similar houses, although a diminishing proportion of the sector was subject to control.[8]

In the post-war period, until 1957, most rents were controlled substantially below current market levels. Between 1939 and 1957 the general retail price index rose by nearly 100 per cent whereas the majority of rents remained frozen at their 1939 levels. Thus the real value of these rents was halved. In fact in certain cases the situation was even more extreme than these figures indicate because the rents were not set at their 1939 market levels, but at the levels prevailing in 1920 or, in some cases, at their 1899 levels![9] Following the 1957 Act approximately 400 000 dwellings (from a stock of about 5 millions) were decontrolled directly, whereas an additional 300 000 were decontrolled in each successive year as they became vacant.[10] For dwellings remaining under control rent increases which would eventually bring their levels up to $2\frac{1}{3}$ times their 1956 gross rateable values were permitted. It might be expected that the behaviour of landlords owning recently decontrolled property would indicate the extent to which their rents had been depressed during the period of control, but no unambiguous picture emerges from studies conducted at the time. For instance, in areas of housing stress – such as certain parts of London – some substantial rent increases were recorded,[11] but in other areas large sectors of the market seem to have been unaffected by the Act. Cullingworth reports that in Lancaster, by 1960, 23 per cent of tenants had had no rent increases at all.[12] However, the fact that not all rents increased should not necessarily be taken to infer an absence of excess demand at the controlled rent level. It may be that the reason for a lack of price response is that not all landlords actively pursue profit-maximisation objectives. Moreover, even if profits do figure among their objectives, or appear as a constraint, the prolonged period of control probably meant that there were substantial lags in the adjustment process.[13]

Finally, since 1965 rents have been subject to regulation once again, but this time on the basis of the fair rent formula laid down in the Act of that year. (A detailed discussion of the formula is presented in the final section of this chapter.) This formula – which is applied to dwellings on the basis of their individual characteristics – has resulted in a wide range of rent changes, both increases and decreases. Table 6.2 shows the distribution of these changes over the period 1966–70. In most cases those dwellings recording very large increases in rent were those which were still controlled under pre-1957 legislation prior to registration, whereas those recording large reductions were free from control prior to 1965. Since 1970 the proportion of rents increased has risen steadily with a resultant increase in the average percentage change to 50 per cent for properties registered for the first time.[14] Clearly, rent regulation has permitted far greater flexibility in the adjustment of rents than previous policies allowed. Moreover, the size of the rent increases suggests greater sensitivity to market conditions than in the past and, as we shall see in the next section, the indications are that rent officers have, albeit unwittingly, used a version of the long-run equilibrium concept in determining fair rent levels.

Overall, therefore, despite the lack of fully comprehensive data, it seems reasonable to conclude that, with the exception of the depression years of 1923–33 and possibly the post-1965 period, controlled rents have usually been set below the long-run equilibrium level. The discrepancy was particularly marked in the post-war period prior to 1957. What effect has this had on the supply of rented accommodation?

The Supply of Rented Housing

Many writers have linked theoretical expectations concerning the effect of rent control to the decline of the privately rented sector, and, indeed, the contemporaneous decline in the size of the rented stock is striking. To illustrate, it is generally thought that at the end of the First World War 90 per cent of the total stock of 7–8 million dwellings were rented from private owners.[15] Throughout the inter-war period the *proportion* of housing that was privately rented fell at an increasing rate, so that by 1947 only about 60 per cent of households rented their dwellings privately – although this still represented about seven million dwellings.[16] Since this time, however, both the proportion and the *absolute size* of the stock have fallen dramatically, so that by 1975 the proportion was less than 16 per cent and accounted for only just over three million dwellings.[17]

However, the causes of this decline are more complex than a simple correlation between rent control and the size (or proportion) of the stock would suggest. First, if we are to identify correctly the role played by rent control we need to separate two distinct supply effects. On the one hand, it may be argued that investors are deterred from making *new* investments in housing because of the low returns it yields; on the other hand, the size of the stock may be depleted as *existing* rental housing is transferred to alternative uses that yield higher returns, notably owner-occupation. Now in the case of the first effect it is questionable whether rent control has been a dominant influence, because, as we explained in the previous section, for the majority of the period under consideration new housing built for renting has been exempt from control. This was the case from 1919 to

TABLE 6.2
Registered rents, England and Wales, 1966—70

(i) Average levels
    Average rent registered   £201 pa
    Average previous rent   £180 pa
    Average percentage change   + 12 per cent
(ii) Distribution of changes

		Percentage	Percentage of total	Numbers
Decreases	> 50	2.7	2 730
	30–49	9.3	9 405
	10–29	13.4	13 619
	< 10	4.7	4 786
No change		8.9	8 986
Increases	< 10	7.2	7 276
	10–29	17.3	17 506
	30–49	11.1	11 200
	50–99	14.2	14 337
	100–199	9.0	9 182
	> 200	2.2	2 279
		100.0	101 306

(iii) Direction of changes

	Percentage			
	1966	1967	1968	169
Total decreases	45	33.6	27.4	24.6
No change	11	8.8	8.9	7.9
Total increases	44	57.9	63.6	67.4

Source: Francis Report (1971) tables 12, 13, p. 25.

1939 and from 1954 to 1965. In fact, it could be argued that controls over a large part of the existing stock may be expected actually to stimulate new building, because the concentration of excess demand on the small uncontrolled sector will mean that prices will be higher there than they would be in the absence of control elsewhere.

Against this view, a criticism of rent control based on its effect on expectations is usually cited. It is pointed out that housing is an extremely durable asset and because of this the investor will have a long time-horizon. If the existence of rent control in one sector of the market is interpreted as increasing the probability that it will be extended to include more recently built property at some time in the future, future returns will need to be discounted more heavily to allow for the increased risk. Hence the expected return on a housing investment will be reduced and, accordingly, appear less attractive. This view first received official sanction when it was cited by the Onslow Committee in 1923 as a reason for the lack of private investment in rental housing.[18] In more recent times the spectre of some future Labour Government fixing unrealistically low rents, or even 'municipalising' rented property, has often been put forward as an explanation of the failure for investment to take place. However, while it is sound practice for the investor to consider the entire time profile of his expected income, and to add a risk premium to his discount factor if he considers future returns to be at risk, there have been, in reality, few examples of the more extreme fears being realised. But in the investors' world rumour is often more potent than reality!

The other supply effect concerns the impact of rent control on the existing stock of housing. The figures quoted on p. 86 show that during the inter-war period there was a relative decline in the size of the stock but not an absolute one. The number of dwellings remained around seven million. Thus although there was a lack of new investment in rental housing, in contrast to the rapid growth in the home occupier and LA sectors, the succession of decontrol policies which gradually freed middle- and higher-valued property from restriction prevented any rapid depletion of the existing stock. After 1945, however, the situation changed markedly. Not only was there a reduction in the proportion of housing rented, but the absolute size of the stock fell as well. A large part of this decline resulted from landlords capitalising their assets by selling their housing for owner-occupation or converting it to non-residential uses. It seems extremely likely that the rigid control of rents which applied until 1957 contributed a great deal towards this transfer. However, the relaxation of restrictions that were introduced in 1957 and 1965 did little to stem the trend. For example, the Milner Holland Committee estimated that in London over the period 1960–3 the loss to the private rented sector through sales was taking place at 2–4 per cent per year.[19] While the process continued more slowly in most other parts of the country, sample studies conducted for the Rowntree Trust[20] and the Social Survey[21] confirm that the national trend was in the same direction. Similarly, figures reported in *Housing and Construction Statistics* show that over one million rented dwellings disappeared in the ten-year period following the 1965 Act.

This failure of subsequent legislation to halt the trend suggests that whatever the effect of rent control, there have been other factors which are important in explaining the decline of the private rented sector; and we shall argue that this is indeed the case. But before doing so, we shall consider the influence of control on the remaining form of investment in housing; that is, conversion, maintenance and repair expenditure. Has rent control deterred landlords from making these expenditures and thereby led to a deterioration in the quality of stock?

The Quality of the Stock

Data collected for 1964 showed that the condition of housing in the private rented sector – as indicated by its possession of basic facilities – was far below that in other tenure groups. Since then three major housing condition sample surveys have confirmed this picture by indicating that the proportion of housing in this sector deemed to be unfit is substantially above that in the owner-occupied and LA categories. The pattern through time is indicated in Table 6.3. To some extent, the relatively poor condition of this housing is a corollary of the lack of investment in new dwellings; for this has meant that the rental stock has an older mean age than other types of housing. (In 1971, the 'Housing Condition Survey' estimated that nearly 70 per cent of private rented housing was built before 1919 compared with less than 35 per cent of the owner-occupied and less than 4 per cent of the LA stock.) However, although unfitness is probably an increasing function of age, maintenance, repair and

TABLE 6.3
Housing condition and amenities by tenure group

	Owner-occupier	Local Authority	Other*
% of dwellings lacking sole use of five basic standard amenities in 1964[1]	39	20	78
% of dwellings unfit in 1967[2]	7	2	33
% of dwellings unfit in 1971[3]	4	1	30
% of dwellings unfit in 1976[4]	3	1	15

* Mainly private rented.
Sources: 1. *The Housing Survey of England and Wales* (1964) table 4.22, p. 78.
2. 'The Housing Condition Survey, England and Wales' (1967), *Economic Trends*, no. 175 (May 1968) table 3, p. 94.
3. 'The Housing Condition Survey, England and Wales' (1971) table 3, p. 13.
4. *English House Condition Survey*, Department of Environment, Press Notice 321 (June 1977).

improvement work can always be used to prevent a good deal of use/time related obsolescence. But the data suggest that it has not been so used.

Once again, therefore, the theoretical predictions seem to have been borne out. (It is interesting, however, to note that for most of the period under review deterioration did not proceed sufficiently far to establish an equilibrium in the controlled sector, judging by the existence of excess demand for controlled property.) Indeed there were a number of reports issued in the 1950s which drew attention to the landlords' inability and/or unwillingness to maintain and repair their property at the low level of controlled rents in force.[22] In fact, it was in response to this pressure that the 1954 Act, which permitted rent increases specifically related to repair and maintenance expenditure, was passed – although it was widely considered that the rent increase formula contained in the Act offered rises that were too low for it to be very effective. However, as we have seen, decontrol was introduced in 1957. But contrary to the expectations of its advocates, it does not seem to have provided a stimulus for a thorough refurbishing of the stock.[23] This tends to suggest that, as in the case of other categories of investment, there have been other factors at work which have also contributed towards the decline of this sector of the housing market. What are these factors?

Investment Finance, Taxation and Consumer Demand

In addition to rent control, three other major contributory factors can be identified in the decline of the private rented sector. Two of these have exerted an influence on the supply of rented housing, whereas the other one has, in the first instance, affected demand conditions. First, as Bowley (1945) has pointed out, the decline of this sector is part of a long-term trend that started at the beginning of the twentieth century as other investment opportunities became available to erstwhile investors in housing. In the period of rapid growth of rented housing which took place in the second half of the nineteenth century, much of the investment finance was provided by small, local savers for whom an investment in property was 'as safe as houses'. However, with the development of the capital market and the growth of financial intermediaries in the twentieth century, these investors had access to alternative investment opportunities which provided equal security and greater liquidity. Hence a major source of housing investment finance was diverted elsewhere.

A second reason for the decline has been the unfavourable tax treatment of the private landlord. In particular, successive governments have taken the view that the extreme durability of housing means that it can be assumed to last 'for ever'. Accordingly, unlike other fixed investment, investment in residential property has not qualified for sinking fund or depreciation tax allowances. This has led Nevitt to conclude that 'the taxing policy of Governments since at least 1878 has been so designed that capital has flowed from rented dwellings into other forms of investment which rate far more favourable tax treatment. The return on rented accommodation has at times been sufficiently high to offset some of the tax disadvantages of holding money in houses, but with increasing levels of taxation the unfavourable treatment has become more serious'.[24]

It could, of course, be conceded that both of these supply-side factors did in fact contribute to the decline of investment in rental housing, but at the same time maintain that if rents were allowed to rise they would have done so sufficiently to offset these adverse effects. However, this view presupposes that the demand for privately rented housing was sufficiently strong to sustain the necessary rent increases. In reality, it is likely that demand was shifting away from the private rented sector for reasons unconnected with rent control. In particular, there was a large growth in the demand for owner-occupied housing and in the provision of Local Authority housing. The growth in home ownership was in part the result of rising incomes and building society finance which made it possible for consumers to realise their preferences for property ownership. But it was also encouraged (in comparison with renting) by favourable property rating practices, the abolition of income tax claims on the owner's imputed income, the tax allowances able to be set against total personal income because of mortgage interest payments, and the absence of any capital gains taxation on profits made through house price appreciation (see Chapter Nine for a discussion of these points). Taken together, these concessions have meant that a higher level of housing consumption can be obtained for a given level of expenditure per period of time by buying instead of renting. Not surprisingly, therefore, the demand for rented accommodation — especially from middle-income groups — has fallen. At the same time, the growth of the Local Authority sector has meant that the demand from lower-income households has also fallen as many of them have been accommodated elsewhere (see Chapter Eight).

Rent Control and Under-Occupation

A third criticism of rent control mentioned earlier is that by reducing the price of housing it stimulates demand and thereby leads to over-consumption or, alternatively, under-occupation. There is certainly some empirical support for this claim. For example,

Table 6.4 shows that according to a survey carried out in 1964, more controlled tenants lived at low densities than any other group, including owner-occupiers. Data for Greater London were particularly striking as they showed that the proportion of controlled tenants living at a density of less than 0.5 persons per room was over twice as large as the proportion of non-controlled tenants. Similarly, on the basis of the 'bedroom standard' (a measure compiled for the survey based on the number, age, sex, and marital status of household members), the table shows that the percentage of controlled tenants enjoying above-average facilities was markedly higher than the percentage of uncontrolled or LA tenants. However, although these figures are consistent with the over-consumption hypothesis, we should be wary in our interpretation of them, for there are many reasons why conditions may vary between tenure groups. For instance, we know that controlled tenancies contain a disproportionately large number of older people who tend to live at lower densities than younger age groups. A fully valid comparison between tenure groups would require standardisation for these and other population differences. Furthermore, we know that housing is a multi-attribute commodity and that space is only one aspect of it.

TABLE 6.4
Density of occupation by tenure groups, 1964

	Owner-occupied	Local Authority	Privately rented Controlled	Privately rented Non-controlled
	%	%	%	%
I Greater London				
Persons per room:				
over 1.5	–	2	2	4
less than 0.5	30	10	33	14
Bedroom standard:				
below standard	4	13	11	20
above standard	65	27	47	29
II Rest of England and Wales				
Persons per room:				
over 1.5	1	3	–	3
less than 0.5	34	14	37	22
Bedroom standard:				
below standard	4	12	8	15
above standard	68	38	60	44

Source: Myra Woolf, *Housing Survey of England and Wales* (H.M.S.O., 1964) table 3.18, p. 62.

There may be other characteristics in the housing vector (particularly qualitative ones) which are less plentiful in controlled property and therefore reduce the overall quantity of services it renders. Certainly De Salvo in his study of rent control in New York City concluded that 'tenants of controlled housing consume neither substantially more nor substantially less housing than similar families in uncontrolled housing; the principal difference is that controlled tenants pay considerably less than the market value for the housing they consume.'[25]

On the other hand, however, information on the price elasticity of demand for housing (quoted in Chapter Four) suggests that it is probably around -0.6: thus, although it is low, it does indicate that demand *will* increase as price falls. Of course, it may be that in certain markets there is no increase in the supply of housing forthcoming at the controlled rent, in which case the demand remains unsatisfied. In the long run, however, it may be expected that tenants whose housing requirements are reduced will have less incentive to economise in their use of housing if they are paying a controlled rent than they would if they were paying higher market prices. Thus although rent control may not stimulate additional demand, it can be expected to reduce the downward adjustments in consumption that would otherwise take place in the later stages of the household's life-cycle.

Income Redistribution

We said at the beginning of this chapter that society's general requirement concerning income redistribution policies is that they should (among other things) transfer income from the more to the less prosperous. Available information about the recipients of the rent regulation 'subsidy' – that is, tenants in private rented accommodation – certainly suggests that they are drawn from the lower-income groups. Table 9.2 (p. 137) shows that the private tenants' category contains a far higher proportion of low-income households than either the LA or owner-occupier categories. For example, in 1975, 20 per cent of private tenant households had an annual income of less than £1000. Hence, according to these data, identifying private tenants as a proxy for low-income groups does seem to have some justification, although like all income proxy measures, there will be many individual exceptions.

As far as landlords are concerned there is no comparable break-down by income class, but there is a certain amount of indirect information which casts doubt on the generality of the popular caricature of the prosperous, cigar-smoking landlord. Figures reported by the Milner Holland Committee show that in London 60 per cent of landlords own only one property, and over 80 per cent own four or less.[26] The predominance of the small landlord is confirmed by the Francis Committee's national sample survey which also shows that 80 per cent of landlords own four properties or less.[27] Now while the possession of a small number of properties in no way establishes that the owner is not a high income earner, it certainly detracts from the view of an oligopolistic market dominated by a few powerful landlords. Moreover, the Francis Committee also found that nearly all landlords had another occupation apart from managing their property, and that they were mainly drawn from Social Classes II (minor professional and managerial) and III (skilled manual). However, this evidence should not be taken to imply that some large organisations do not exist within the privately rented market – indeed, Milner Holland found that 32 per cent of *lettings* were supplied by organisations with over one hundred properties – but, rather, that there is considerable heterogeneity among landlords. Given this fact, an income-transfer policy based on property ownership is likely to be highly imperfect.

Rent Regulation

The 1965 Rent Act restored a measure of control to a large part of the privately rented sector by introducing a system of rent regulation. This policy, which is still in operation at the present time (1978), was designed to reconcile the needs of the tenant requiring protection from excessive rents, particularly in areas of housing stress, with those of the landlord seeking an acceptable return on his investment. The fundamental difference between regulation and earlier policies of control is that it involves fixing a 'fair rent' for each property on the basis of its individual characteristics. Furthermore, there is provision for periodic rent reviews which enable rents to be adjusted to bring them up to date.

Given the multiple causes of the long-run decline in the private rented sector it was most unlikely that this policy, on its own, would have a marked effect on this trend. And this expectation has indeed been borne out. In the ten years following the Act's implementation the stock of rented dwellings has fallen by over a million until it now represents less than 16 per cent of the total housing stock. The Francis Committee summarised the supply situation as follows: 'there can be little doubt that the broad picture is a gloomy one. The supply of private unfurnished accommodation for renting is continuing to diminish. It would be wrong to attribute this solely or even mainly to rent regulation. The trend was there before the Rent Act of 1965, and indeed before 1957. Neither the Rent Act of 1957 nor the Act of 1965 did anything to halt it. The inference seems to be that this trend is largely due to the advantages of, and the widespread desire for, owner occupation.'[28] However, although the Act may not merit attention because of any marked impact it has had upon the supply of accommodation, it is of interest to the economist because of its curious attempt to specify a 'fair rent' on the basis of an explicit formula.

Section 27 of the 1965 Act (subsequently consolidated in later Acts) defined the fair rent formula as follows:

1. In determining for the purposes of this Part of the Act what rent is or would be a fair rent under a regulated tenancy of a dwelling house, regard shall be had, subject to the following provisions of this section, to all the circumstances (other than personal circumstances) and in particular to the age, character and locality of the dwelling house and to its state of repair.

2. For the purposes of the determination it shall be assumed that the number of persons seeking to become tenants of similar dwelling houses in the locality on the terms (other than those relating to rent) of the regulated tenancy is not substantially greater than the number of such dwelling houses in the locality which are available for letting on such terms.

Despite the apparent precision of this formula, the theoretical foundations of the concept are extremely dubious. One writer – with whom most economists would probably agree – has described it simply as 'theoretical nonsense'.[29] Some clarification of the principles involved may have been expected from the Francis Committee, but far from clarifying the issues, they actively contributed to the confusion surrounding the subject by presenting a set of arguments so convoluted that they deserve to become required reading for every beginning student who needs to be made aware of the pitfalls that abound in elementary economic analysis.[30] Let us, therefore, try to make some sense of Section 27.

The first paragraph states that the characteristics of the dwelling, including its locality, are the relevant criteria for assessing a fair rent. Although the ability of the existing tenant to pay this rent (that is, his personal circumstances) is specifically excluded from consideration, these are none the less the same features that would be relevant if the rent was determined within the market. The second paragraph, however, instructs the Rent Officer to assume, for purposes of valuation, that the number of dwellings in the locality is roughly equal to the number of tenants seeking accommodation *irrespective of the amount of rent they are willing and able to pay.* It is this procedure – which has been described as a means for establishing what the market price would be in the absence of scarcity – that has caused so much consternation.

It is likely that the architects of this section had in their minds the concept of housing need: that is, the quantity of housing required to supply a given population with a minimum standard of accommodation, disregarding their ability to pay for it. However, if the satisfaction of need is used as a basis for price determination, and households vary in the amount they are willing and able to pay in rent, then the fair rent will be set at the level which the marginal or last household is able to pay. Even if we assume that the marginal household is willing and able to pay a non-zero rent, so that the demand schedule is kinked and becomes totally inelastic at the point where need is satisfied (as in Figure 6.3), it is most unlikely – given our knowledge of the income levels of the poorer households in stress areas – that the fair rent will correspond to a long-run equilibrium rent. Thus in Figure 6.3 the long-run equilibrium rent r^* is shown to be

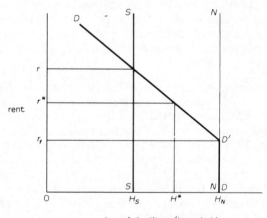

Figure 6.3   Stock equilibrium and fair rents

below the short-run market rent r, but above the fair rent, r_f, which would be established if the stock of dwellings, SS, was increased to a level at which need, NN, was satisfied. (This also assumes, of course, that additional tenants are not attracted into the area by the existence of low rents.)[31]

Clearly such a formula has major shortcomings as a basis for rent determination. Among them we may note that in common with other forms of rent control discussed previously it may be expected to exacerbate housing shortages as the stock of dwellings declines. The Institute of Rent Officers obviously recognised these inconsistencies and in their submission to the Francis Committee they sought to have paragraph (2) redefined so that it refers to an equality between the number of dwellings and the number of would-be tenants at *the fair rent*.[32] (Although even with this modification, for both paragraphs (1) and (2) to be satisfied, and for the fair rent to be a long-run equilibrium one, it would be necessary to provide those households who could not afford the fair rent level ($0H_N - 0H^*$) with purchasing power so that their needs could be registered.) However, the Committee appear to have failed to grasp the significance of this proposal and rejected it. Nevertheless, it is likely that this interpretation approximates more closely the original intentions of the drafters of the legislation and certainly, in practice, rent levels appear to have been set with this view in mind; or, at least, far above the minimum levels that a precise interpretation of paragraph (2) would imply.[33]

CHAPTER SEVEN

Slums and Urban Renewal

Slum housing is an all-too-familiar part of the British housing scene. In 1976 the *English House Condition Survey* estimated that nearly 800,000 dwellings were unfit for habitation: this represents nearly 5 per cent of the housing stock. When dwellings lacking one or more basic amenity are added to these, the proportion of substandard housing rises to nearly 9 per cent of the stock (see Table 2.1 (p. 17)). In many cases the problems associated with this housing are accentuated because it is heavily concentrated in particular areas; typically, parts of the older, inner areas of the nation's towns and cities. A stroll around the London Boroughs of Lambeth and Southwark; of Moss Side in Manchester, or the near-by town of Salford; or Granby in Liverpool or the West End district of Newcastle; or any other one of the numerous older inner-city areas in Britain will indicate quite vividly the extent of the problem. In this chapter we shall focus our attention on these urban concentrations of slum housing by looking at their causes and policies for their renewal.[1]

Economic Theories of Slum Creation

It is possible to identify two major processes that have resulted in the creation of slum housing conditions. The first of these involves changes in the pattern of demand through time which have led to the growth of new suburban areas and the associated decline of parts of the inner city. This process has been aptly summarised by Ratcliff (1949) in the following manner:

> Neighborhoods of new houses pass through a predictable cycle as the structures deteriorate and become obsolete and as the original families grow and decline. The houses become less attractive with age, costs of upkeep rise, and repairs are neglected. The predominance of home ownership declines as families move away or are dissolved and as foreclosure is followed by tenancy . . . Values fall, and structures are converted to small apartments or to commercial uses. As the neighborhoods deteriorate, they are unattractive to young families, whose housing needs are typically satisfied by new dwellings, and the areas are abandoned to lower income groups.[2]

In this description, emphasis is placed upon the fall in demand for inner-city housing on the part of high- and middle-income groups who move to the suburbs and leave their previous housing to low-income households. Some of the factors which can be expected to lead to this fall in demand are: transport improvements providing easier access to the central city from the suburbs, changing preferences favouring new styles of housing and lower residential densities, and the decentralisation of many job locations. At the same time these demand factors are reinforced by certain cost changes. For example, the rising maintenance and repair costs associated with older housing, together with the frequent intrusion of commercial and other activities which impose external costs on city residents, tend to raise the relative price of inner-city housing *vis-à-vis* suburban housing. As this urban housing is vacated it becomes available to lower-income groups. (It is, therefore, a filtering process – see Chapter Three.) However, their limited purchasing power does not permit them to consume it in its original form. Thus landlords tend to subdivide properties into the smaller units that they can afford. This often results in multiple occupation and overcrowding, which is a well-known source of accelerated property deterioration.

The above cycle has been particularly pronounced in the United States where many inner-city areas have been completely abandoned by the white middle classes and now comprise almost totally low-income, ethnic minority groups. While this phenomenon has been less widespread in Britain, there are none the less a number of areas, especially in London, where erstwhile middle-class housing has been vacated by those income groups for whom it was built originally, and subdivided into smaller units for low-income households – often with an associated marked decline in the quality of the housing. But possibly an equally (if not more) important source of slum housing in Britain is what we may term 'purpose-built'. This is the second process to which we referred above.

Whereas some housing may be built originally to acceptable standards but deteriorate through time because of conversion and lack of maintenance and repair work, much of the older unfit housing in Britain was built to standards that today would be considered inadequate. Such housing (of which large amounts can still be seen in many industrial towns of the North) was built during the nineteenth century to house the rapidly expanding urban industrial workforce. Because their earnings were insufficient to enable them to afford good-quality dwellings, large quantities of cheap terraced (often back-to-back) housing were constructed to accommodate them. As this housing was substandard by present-day standards of construction and amenities at the time it was built, it is hardly surprising that the passage of time has exacerbated its deficiencies.

There are therefore at least two ways in which slum housing conditions may be produced. Both of them, however, rest upon the fact that such housing depends upon the demand from low-income groups who are unable to afford anything better.[3] This clear association of poor-quality slum housing with low-income tenants has led Muth (1969) to assert that slums are but one result of general poverty. Just as poor families are often unable to obtain adequate food and clothing, so they are unable to obtain adequate housing. The significance of this viewpoint is that it rejects the claim that slum housing results from the malfunctioning of the housing market. Indeed, it is sometimes argued that slums represent an optimal response to low-income demand! Against this view, others have argued that the formation of areas of slum housing often depends upon additional factors which do suggest that the housing market operates inefficiently as well as inequitably.

Rothenberg (1967), for example, has pointed out that there are likely to be market imperfections affecting both demand and supply conditions which contribute towards the formation and continued existence of slum housing. On the demand side, there are a number of factors which lead to a strong inelastic demand for slum housing even though its *price per unit of services* may be higher than better-quality housing.[4] For example, slum tenants are frequently ill-informed about alternative housing opportunities and their prices. We saw in Chapter One that lack of information is likely to affect all groups within the housing market, but slum dwellers are often particularly disadvantaged in this respect. This may be because they have only recently arrived in a city and have not had sufficient time to acquire the necessary information, or it may be that lack of education or familiarity with the housing system means that they do not know how to acquire it. On other occasions, tenants' immobility may be exacerbated by the presence of racial or other forms of discrimination (such as limitations on their access to credit) which make it difficult for them to obtain housing outside their existing neighbourhoods. Yet another impediment to their mobility is presented through the combined effect of job locations and commuting costs. In many cities it is the centrally located service industries which provide employment for low-skilled workers. The low incomes these workers receive do not permit them to undertake expensive commuting trips and they are therefore forced to look for housing in close proximity to their work. Hence they tend to be confined to inner-city housing areas.

On the supply side of the market, indivisibilities in the supply of better-quality housing usually place its minimum quantities beyond the budgets of low-income groups, even though (as we have argued above) the price per unit they pay for slum housing is sometimes above the price per unit paid for better-quality housing. Thus there are economies of scale in housing consumption. (In the United States these indivisibilities are often generated by land-use planning regulations which specify minimum plot sizes or other minimum standard constraints which are used as exclusionary devices against low-income groups.)

The existence of neighbourhood externalities may also be a source of supply-side inefficiency leading to a lack of maintenance and repair expenditure and a consequent deterioration of the property within an area. This effect is likely to be particularly pronounced on the borders of slum areas where the decision whether to maintain a property in a good state of repair, or to allow it to deteriorate in the same way as adjoining properties, is often faced. It is therefore important in explaining the way in which slums spread. In essence the mechanism works as follows: because the value of a property depends not only upon its own physical features and condition, but also on those of other properties in the vicinity, it is possible that a landlord (or owner) will be deterred from improving his own property because of the fear that his returns will be jeopardised by the external costs imposed on his property by unimproved adjoining ones. Because each landlord is faced with this uncertainty about his neighbour's likely activities, no one will be willing to risk investing in maintenance and repair work. However, if they all *did* invest, both they and society in general would probably be better off. This is the classic 'prisoner's dilemma' which has been applied to the housing market by Davis and Whinston (1961). Let us look a little more closely at the way it operates by using a numerical example.

To simplify matters let us assume that there are just two landlords, Crown and Church, who own two adjacent properties and who are each considering investing in repair work. If neither landlord knows whether or not the other one is going to invest, neither can be sure of the return he would receive, but each one can identify four possible combinations of strategies, and the returns he would receive in each case. These are summarised for each landlord in the 'pay-off' matrix shown in Figure 7.1.

The left-hand entry in each cell refers to Crown's return. Thus if he invests while Church also invests he obtains a 7 per cent return; if, on the other hand, he doesn't invest while Church does, he benefits – via the external effect which increases the value of his property – without any expenditure, and thereby makes a higher return of 10 per cent.[5] If Crown invests while Church doesn't, he obtains a lower return than he would have done if they both invested, because of the negative externality imposed on his property by Church's non-repaired

Church:

		Invest		Don't invest	
Crown:	Invest	7	7	3	10
	Don't invest	10	3	4	4

Figure 7.1 Rates of return on maintenance expenditure (%)

property. Finally, if Crown decides not to invest and Church does likewise, he obtains a 4 per cent return which is lower than he would receive if they both invested, but more than he would receive if he alone invested. This particular matrix has been constructed on the assumption that these interdependencies are symmetrical and so Church faces an identical set of outcomes dependent upon Crown's actions. Now if he is confronted with these possibilities, how will Crown react? First, he may assume that Church *will* invest, in which case it pays him *not* to do so because in this way he would make a 10 rather than a 7 per cent return. Alternatively, he may assume that Church will *not* invest: in this case he will once again maximise his return by *not* investing. Thus in both cases, Crown will make a larger return by not investing. Similar reasoning will show that Church will reach the same conclusion. Accordingly, when both landlords act independently, and are unsure of the other's actions, they will decide not to invest although they (and society) would have been better off if they had both decided to invest!

Of course, the question 'Why don't the two landlords collaborate and thereby reach the optimal combination?' immediately arises. In our two-person, two-property example such collaboration would seem to be a likely outcome. However, in reality, a slum neighbourhood will comprise a large number of landlords which would make co-operation and agreement far more difficult to achieve, especially when there is always an incentive for any one landlord to renege on an agreement and thereby increase his personal return.

Alternatively, if co-operation cannot be relied upon, one might expect an individual landlord to acquire a number of properties and repair them all, and thereby realise the higher returns obtainable on adjoining improved properties; that is, 'internalise the externalities'. However, once again, the difficulties involved in acquiring numerous properties from different owners tend to make this outcome unlikely. This is especially true if individual owners recognise the property assembly process going on, for they can be expected to try to extract the maximum price from the buyer, which would – in the limit – eliminate any surplus the buyer might expect to realise. Thus we may conclude that atomistic behaviour is likely to prevail and to lead to an inefficient outcome. Of course, whether or not the external effects are, in fact, strong enough to bring about the predicted outcome is an empirical question which can only be tested in the light of actual events.

Finally, on the question of externalities, it should also be pointed out that the view of slum housing as an optimal market response to low-income demand tends to ignore a more general set of external costs that are usually associated with slum housing conditions. For example, poor health, fire risks and a higher-than-average propensity for slum dwellers to engage in crime are just some of the ways in which these costs may manifest themselves. When health, fire and crime prevention services are provided publicly, and financed from taxation revenues, taxpayers in general will find themselves bearing some of these (often unquantifiable) costs of slum housing.[6]

To conclude this part of our discussion on the causes of slum housing, we may say that some authors have stressed the inadequate purchasing power of slum dwellers who cannot afford decent housing whereas others have emphasised the part played by various market imperfections. The distinction is of some importance to the subject of policy choice decisions. The former outlook suggests that a general policy of income supplementation – which raises the incomes of slum dwellers to a level which enables them to buy an acceptable minimum quantity of housing services – will in the long run be the most efficient way of eliminating slums. The market-imperfections interpretation, on the other hand, will require some form of intervention in the housing market to overcome or remove specific imperfections.

Of course, one does not have to choose one theory and reject the other: it is quite possible that both sets of influences have played a part in the formation of slums, in which case elements of both policies will be necessary to eliminate them. Thus government-backed schemes for urban renewal represent one specifically housing market response to the problem, although these will need to be combined with financial provisions which assist low-income groups, since otherwise they would not be able to afford the better-quality replacement housing – see Chapters Eight and Nine for a discussion of this point.

Government Policies Towards Slums

As far as the first component of the policy is concerned (that is, the actual replacement of slum housing) two major types of programme may be identified. First, there has been a policy of general redevelopment which has proceeded under the auspices of the 'slum-clearance programme'. Essentially, this has been concerned with the demolition and replacement of areas of unfit housing. It has been carried out by Local Authorities, which since the 1930s have been able to designate 'clearance areas' where there are two or more adjacent houses which are deemed unfit for habitation. Once an area has been so designated the LA can acquire the property – ultimately by compulsory purchase order if the need arises–and demolish it to allow redevelopment of the site. In addition, rather wider powers for redevelopment schemes are conferred on LAs by the various Planning Acts. These enable them to declare 'comprehensive redevelopment areas' within which they are able to acquire property – both fit and unfit – if their overall planning strategy requires large-scale redevelopment. This redevelopment may be undertaken by the LA or a private developer; in the case of housing, the LA has usually retained ownership of the land and acted as the contractor for development and, thereafter, the landlord.

Since 1969, however, there has been a shift of emphasis from programmes involving redevelopment to those favouring rehabilitation. In fact, rehabilitation policy was officially sanctioned as long ago as 1949 when LAs were first empowered to offer grants towards the cost of improving or converting substandard houses. But the take-up rate of these grants was very low.[7] In 1959 the policy was strengthened with the introduction of standard mandatory grants for the installation of basic amenities (fixed bath, wash-hand basin, sink, WC, and hot and cold water at three points) and discretionary grants for other prescribed improvement work. But, once again, the take-up rate was low and official policy continued to place stress on redevelopment work until the 1969 Housing Act.

A number of factors can be identified as contributing towards this change of policy direction. First, there was a widespread and growing unease with the wholesale demolition of established communities that redevelopment often entailed.[8] Second, the volume of resources available to be devoted to redevelopment was insufficient to bring about the desired increase in the quality of the housing stock in an acceptable period of time, given the number of substandard dwellings and the rate at which fit dwellings were deteriorating. Moreover, as a large proportion of substandard housing was privately owned it was hoped that improvement policy would attract additional private resources to the task of renovation. Finally, it was expected that a given quantity of resources would distribute benefits more widely if they were used for renovation work than they would if they were devoted to redevelopment (Kirwan and Martin, 1972).

Alongside the shift of emphasis towards rehabilitation explicit recognition was given to the fact that the neighbourhood environment constitutes an important housing externality. Accordingly, the 1969 Act gave LAs the power to designate 'general improvement areas' in which property improvement could be complemented by expenditures on the environment: pedestrianisation schemes, road improvements, landscaping and other cosmetic devices fall within the scope of this policy (see Smith, 1974).

This is but a brief sketch of the general directions that renewal policy has taken in Britain in recent years. Obviously any policy involving large expenditures and affecting such a fundamental aspect of life as housing conditions and the shape of the urban environment will tend to generate intense debate. Not surprisingly, therefore, there is a voluminous literature on the subject – economists, politicians, sociologists, geographers and many others have all made contributions.[9] From this diverse and rich menu we have selected one area in which economists have been able to make a distinctive contribution to the debate. This concerns the role of evaluation in the urban renewal process.

Economic Evaluation of Urban Renewal

The general principles governing the decision whether to renew a single property (either by redevelopment or renovation) or to leave it in an unchanged state are reasonably well-defined. A view needs to be taken about the benefits and costs likely to arise over the remaining lifetime of the existing property, and these need to be compared with the costs (both capital and operating) and benefits likely to arise from a renewed building over its, typically longer, lifetime. To facilitate this comparison the cost and benefit streams need to be discounted and expressed in present value terms. If the expected net present value of the renewed building is shown to be greater than the net present value of the building in its existing form then renewal becomes worth while. This decision rule can be expressed formally in terms of the conventional net present value formula as follows:

$$\text{NPV}_o = \sum_{t=1}^{n-j} \frac{B_{ot} - C_{ot}}{(1+i)^t}, \qquad \text{where } 1 < j < n \tag{7.1}$$

$$\text{NPV}_1 = \sum_{t=1}^{n} \frac{B_{1t} - C_{1t}}{(1+i)^t} \tag{7.2}$$

Proceed with renewal if $\text{NPV}_1 > \text{NPV}_0$

where NPV_0 = net present value of existing building
  NPV_1 = net present value of renewed building
  B_{0t} = benefit from existing building in its tth year
  B_{1t} = benefit from renewed building in its tth year
  C_{0t} = cost of existing building in its tth year
  C_{1t} = cost of renewed building in its tth year
  i = discount rate

If the renewal decision involves redevelopment, the costs of this option will include demolition and site preparation costs, as well as the construction costs of a new building and its annual maintenance and repair costs. On the other hand, a decision to continue to use a building in its existing form will just involve maintenance and repair costs, albeit probably at a somewhat higher level. Understandably, therefore, the initial cost of renewal will only be justified if the additional annual benefits are sufficiently great and/or the extra life of the renewed building is long enough to offset these capital costs. When measuring the benefits, the private landlord will be concerned with his annual rental income, although from the public sector's point of view considerations of consumer surplus and externalities may well mean that rent is an inadequate measure of social benefit. (This point is discussed further below.)

Once suitable measures for each of the variables in the NPV formula have been obtained, the decision rule indicates whether renewal will be worth while. However, the choice facing an LA is rarely of this form. More frequently, statutory minimum housing standards are used to determine whether or not a dwelling is fit for habitation, and if it is found to be defective some form of action is required. The dwelling cannot continue to be used in its present form even if it appears profitable to do so. Moreover, if land requirements suggest the desirability of renewal rather than abandonment then the question becomes: 'What form of renewal should be chosen?' As we have mentioned already, the evidence of recent years shows a distinct policy shift away from renewal schemes involving redevelopment towards those favouring rehabilitation. Interestingly, some of the reasons for this shift of emphasis can be shown to emerge from an adaptation of the preceding decision rule. This has been demonstrated by Needleman (1965).

Needleman argues that an LA faced with the choice of rebuilding or renovating has, in essence, the option of incurring a large capital cost in the immediate future (via rebuilding) or of delaying this capital expenditure, by extending the life of the existing dwelling (through a smaller renovation expenditure), and undertaking the rebuilding at a later date. Furthermore, by assuming that the relative benefit flows associated with each option are unimportant as long as they both provide at least an acceptable minimum standard of housing (a pragmatic approach resulting partly from the difficulty of measuring benefits which Needleman modifies somewhat at a later stage – see below), the decision rule is converted into one involving cost minimisation. That is, which option involves the smaller cost in present value terms? The main factors which will determine the answer to this question are: the relative capital costs of rebuilding and renovation, their relative annual running costs, the length of life of the renovated building, and the discount rate. Formally, we may say that renovation will be the preferred option if:

$$b > m + b(1 + i)^{-\lambda} + \frac{r}{i}(1 - \{1 + i\}^{-\lambda}), \qquad (7.3)$$

where b = cost of demolition, site preparation and rebuilding
m = cost of renovation
$b(1 + i)^{-\lambda}$ = present value of rebuilding in λ years, discounted at $i\%$
λ = life of renovated property in years
r = difference in annual running costs of rebuilt and renovated property[10]

The probability of renovation being revealed as the preferred strategy will tend to increase as the cost of renovation in relation to rebuilding falls, the life of the renovated property increases, the excess running costs associated with renovation fall and the discount rate rises. The last factor will be important because as the discount rate rises the incentive to postpone present-day expenditures until the (more heavily discounted) future will become stronger.

Following comments by Sigsworth and Wilkinson (1967, 1970) on his initial formulation of this decision rule, Needleman (1968, 1969) refined his formula to allow for the possibility of increases in the real costs of rebuilding through time and differences in relative benefit levels derived by tenants in new and renovated property. Increases in building costs can be dealt with by simply including a factor (z) which represents the annual increase in replacement costs. Relative benefit levels, on the other hand, are more problematic. In the absence of any readily available measure of the amount of benefit yielded by alternative types of accommodation, Needleman uses the difference in rent level (p) as a surrogate. With these two refinements the amended formula becomes:

$$b > m + b\frac{(1+z)^{\lambda}}{1+i} + \frac{r+p}{i}(1 - \{1+i\}^{-\lambda}). \qquad (7.4)$$

The introduction of these two additional terms tends to reduce the probability of renovation being preferred to rebuilding, other factors remaining equal.

Finally, one complication of considerable practical importance dealt with by Needleman concerns situations where renewal of an extensive area is planned. In such cases the property involved is often of mixed quality: some is usually capable of renovation, whereas some is often too dilapidated to permit rehabilitation and requires demolition and rebuilding. However, if a mixed strategy of renovation and rebuilding is adopted, the average cost per rebuilt dwelling will tend to increase as the proportion of renovated properties increases, because – among other things – redevelopment economies of scale will be impaired. The form of this cost relationship may be expressed as follows:

$$B = b + g\left\{1 - \frac{C}{T}\right\}, \qquad (7.5)$$

where B = average cost per rebuilt dwelling
b = average cost per rebuilt dwelling, assuming 100 per cent rebuilding
T = total number of dwellings within the renewal area
C = number of dwellings cleared for rebuilding.

Thus when total clearance and rebuilding takes place $\frac{C}{T} = 1$ and the average cost per rebuilt dwelling is equal to b. As the number of renovated dwellings increases so an additional cost, represented by the function g, is incurred. The question to be resolved is therefore whether it is worth while undertaking a mixed strategy, with some lower renovation costs and some higher average rebuilding costs, or whether total redevelopment with lower unit rebuilding costs should be pursued. When the rebuilding cost relationship is incorporated into the basic formula it reveals that, *ceteris paribus*, the higher the proportion of dwellings to be cleared the less attractive partial renovation becomes compared with total redevelopment.

Decision rules of the type described above have now been developed to a stage where they provide a succinct and well-defined yardstick for LA decision-making. It must be stressed, however, that in the process of constructing a manageable rule for general application, many of the diverse manifestations of a renewal decision – with which an LA is typically called upon to deal – are either omitted from consideration or dealt with in a somewhat cursory fashion. Among these the whole question of the benefit levels to be obtained from renewal schemes clearly warrants far more attention. One approach which provides a possible line of advance in this direction lies in the application of more general cost-benefit analysis techniques to the housing case.

Cost-Benefit Analysis in Housing Project Evaluation

Social cost-benefit analysis is now a well-established technique for evaluating public sector projects. It is particularly suitable when public goods are produced, as these cannot be priced in the normal way, and when the incidence of external costs and benefits means that market prices are a poor indicator of social welfare. In essence, it involves the identification, enumeration and evaluation of the entire range of social costs and benefits (that is, private *and* external costs and benefits) associated with a project, so that a social rate-of-return or benefit-cost ratio can be computed. Such a procedure will assist the decision-maker in his choice of projects by indicating to him whether or not a particular project will yield an adequate return, and/or enabling him to rank a set of alternative projects.[11]

Although the technique has been used widely in some areas, notably in the field of transport project appraisal, its application to housing investments has to date been rather limited. Nevertheless, the principles are clear and an extension of its use in this area seems likely as decision-makers involved in housing matters become more familiar with the approach. Accordingly let us proceed by considering some of the main methodological issues in the context of a housing redevelopment scheme.

In any scheme we may identify three main categories of costs and benefits. First, there will be the direct costs and benefits which accrue to the producers and users of the new housing. Second, there will be neighbourhood externalities which will be experienced by residents and others in the areas near to the redeveloped site. Finally, there will be a range of more general external benefits associated with the improved living conditions of renewed housing. These will include reduced expenditures on health care and crime prevention which, we have argued previously, will be reaped by society at large and so we shall refer to them as 'societal externalities'. Let us consider each of these categories more closely. As we have already devoted some attention to the measurement and evaluation of costs, here we shall concentrate on the more complicated subject of the benefits which renewal schemes produce.

The way in which the direct benefits arise and are measured will depend upon the role of the government in the renewal process. In the United States, for example, the government restricts its role to site acquisition and preparation; the cleared site is then sold to private developers, who undertake the rebuilding. By its intervention the government is overcoming the obstacle to renewal presented by the 'prisoner's dilemma' which we discussed in an earlier section. Hence the benefit from its action, which would not otherwise be achieved by the private market, arises from the internalisation of externalities. As Rothenberg puts it:

> Under fragmented tenure, land use is sub-optimal because co-ordination or integration across tenure plots is unavailable. The land itself has lower productivity than it might have because the barrier of fragmented ownership forces it to be used in units that are too small. Government assembly for redevelopment incurs all the costs of assembly, demolition, clearance and site preparation in order to create what is in effect a new type of land input — land that can be used in units large enough to internalize neighborhood externalities. It is as if a technical innovation were made, transforming all units of a certain input to ones with higher productivity. This virtual input transformation is the source of externality benefits. It represents net social gain in terms of national income.[12]

Thus it is argued that government intervention raises the productivity of land. Moreover Rothenberg goes on to argue that this enhanced productivity can be valued in terms of the pre- and post-clearance land prices. Ultimately, of course, the land price will be paid for by the users of the redeveloped site and so this view implies that the level of benefit they receive is measured by this price. Now this approach is, of course, very similar to the one adopted by Needleman, who also argued that relative benefit levels may be represented by consumer payments – in his case, different rent levels. However, it should be pointed out that in his analysis Rothenberg draws a distinction between the benefit which is measured by the increased land value, which derives from the internalisation of externalities, and any benefit which arises from the new building on the land. In his view the latter category should not be included as a benefit of the redevelopment scheme *per se* because, he argues, if there is full employment it simply represents the displacement of resources which would have yielded equal benefit elsewhere.

In Britain, as we have seen, LAs typically perform a larger role in the development process: not only do they assume responsibility for site acquisition and preparation, but they are often directly involved in the building process and, in cases where council housing is built, they retain a continuing interest in the property through their role as landlords. In these circumstances there is no market transaction involving the sale of land and buildings on which a benefit measure could be based. The LA will, however, receive rent payments from its tenants, and, as we have seen, these are often used to evaluate benefits. But we have already expressed reservations about the use of such measures. A major reason for this dissatisfaction is that rent payments are likely to produce a systematic underestimate of the actual level of benefit received because they do not take account of the tenants' consumer surplus, that is, the difference between the amount that tenants would be willing to pay for their housing and the actual amount they are required to pay. This underestimation is likely to occur whenever a uniform rent measure common to a large group of tenants is used (because intra-marginal users are usually willing to pay more than marginal users), but it will tend to be especially large in the case of LA rents which are administered and set below the market level.

To illustrate this point consider the situation depicted in Figure 7.2, where initially a stock of LA housing, $0H_1$, is let at a uniform rent level, $0r$. This rent is below the market level and so an excess demand for LA housing exists. Consequently, when a new development that increases the stock to $0H_2$ is completed, this additional housing can be let at the same rent. However, if the rental income is taken as a measure of the benefits accruing to the tenants of this housing it will understate the true measure by an amount equal to the shaded portion in Figure 7.2.[13] Clearly, a superior measure would be one based on the total amount tenants would be willing to pay. But how could such a measure be obtained?

One approach used relatively recently in a rather different context was that employed by the research team examining possible sites for

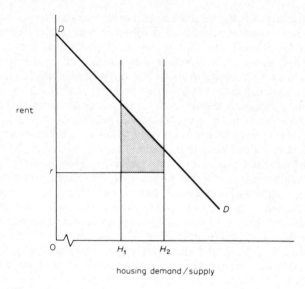

Figure 7.2   Local Authority rents and consumer surplus

the proposed Third London Airport.[14] They were concerned to measure the quantity of consumer surplus received by existing residents in the areas they examined, as this would be lost if the residents were forced to move because of aircraft noise. Accordingly they adopted a survey procedure in which they asked a sample of households the minimum compensation they would require if they had to move from their houses because of a redevelopment scheme, such that they would be as well-off after the move as before it. In this way it was hoped to obtain an estimate of the value each household attached to living in their house. That is, the value they placed on the total benefit they received from living there, which when compared with its market value would yield an estimate of their consumer surplus. Although this procedure is formally correct, and should produce the desired results, it does involve a number of drawbacks. Notably it is based on consumer opinions instead of market behaviour: an approach about which most economists are sceptical because they believe that people are less adept at, or devote less attention to, valuation procedures in these settings compared with ones when actual expenditures are made. Indeed, 8 per cent of the sample interviewed in connection with the London Airport project said that no level of compensation whatsoever would be sufficient to compensate them for moving. Unless one is prepared to accept the possibility of an infinite level of benefit being produced by a particular dwelling, this finding confirms the economists' reservations about opinion surveys. Hence the researcher is faced with a dilemma: market prices/rents are known to provide inaccurate measures of tenants'/owners' benefits but at present no completely satisfactory alternative method of valuation exists. The same problem emerges when the neighbourhood and societal external benefits are considered.

Neighbourhood externalities may arise in areas adjoining the renewal site because the proximity of better-quality housing makes these areas more attractive than they were when slums were located near by. Similarly, if improved housing conditions reduce the tendency for erstwhile slum tenants to suffer certain types of ill health associated with poor housing, such as colds, bronchitis, typhoid, etc., or reduce their tendency to engage in crime and other anti-social activities, then, to the extent that society in general has to devote fewer resources to health care and crime prevention, an external societal benefit accrues (or, more accurately, there has been a reduction in external societal costs). Of course, this is a rather blunt reference to a subject of great complexity and it should not be taken to imply that the process of causality, or the precise relationship between housing investment and the alleviation of external societal costs, is precise or straightforward. Clearly this is not the case. But there are probably few people who would deny that there *is* a relationship between housing conditions and these factors, and so to ignore them would produce an underestimate of benefit levels. However, the problem of valuation persists.

Once again, market indicators in the form of enhanced property values have been used to evaluate the improved environmental conditions resulting from neighbourhood externalities. As we have seen, this is an imperfect procedure but the treatment of societal externalities is even more problematic. A possible approach is to value them by looking at the reduction in avoidance costs resulting from housing improvements. Thus information on the incidence of different types of illness between slum and non-slum dwellers – and the associated health care costs – may be used to estimate the long-run reduction in health care expenditure that may be expected to follow improvements in housing conditions. Similarly reductions in crime and other anti-social activities could, in principle, be valued by using reductions in policing costs. Clearly, however, these procedures involve enormous problems and we could not be confident of producing a high degree of precision.

In fact, this verdict is probably true of many of the valuation stages in cost-benefit analysis: we are able to identify, and possibly measure in non-monetary units, most of the categories of costs and benefits, but our attempts at valuation leave much to be desired. Recognition of this fact has led Lichfield *et al* (1975) to develop a modified evaluative approach which retains the rigour of a cost-benefit framework, by identifying and measuring all the categories of costs and benefits associated with a project, but which concedes that – given the current state of evaluation techniques – some items will not be amenable to exact valuation.

In such cases it may be possible to rank projects in terms of the general magnitudes of particular non-quantified items (that is, use an ordinal rather than a cardinal measure), or to express them in terms of a more limited set of inequalities, or simply to note the incidence of non-quantifiable effects. For example, a recent study carried out by Brighton Council used the Lichfield approach to examine the relative merits of redeveloping and rehabilitating an estate of old council housing.[15] Among the items which were not able to be quantified but were able to be ranked between projects were the costs of community disruption, the benefits of an improved environment and the benefits of LA tenants receiving a housing type of their choice. Each of these items was considered to vary sufficiently between the six policy options to permit ranking. Other social factors, such as the disruption of existing social networks and support systems, were identified but the differential effects associated with each project were not considered amenable to ranking.

To make an unambiguous choice between projects it would of course be necessary to aggregate the costs and benefits associated with each item – a procedure that is clearly not possible when there is no common unit of measurement. Thus a unique solution will not emerge from the Lichfield approach except in the unlikely event that one project is superior to all the alternatives in every aspect. Nevertheless, what the procedure does provide – by its use of a 'planning balance sheet' in which all the cost and benefit items are recorded – is a framework for decision-making in which the full ramifications of each project are identified. The less tangible neighbourhood and societal externalities will, therefore, be brought to the attention of the decision-makers, who will, ultimately, need to use their personal judgements in comparing them with other items. But this is entirely as it should be: the approach is an aid to the political process of decision-making, *not* a substitute for it.[16]

Finally, one other distinct advantage of the Lichfield approach should be stressed. This concerns the income distributional aspects of a project. By using a balance-sheet format it is possible to identify each group affected by a project – whether as a producer or consumer, a beneficiary or a loser. Thus, in the Brighton project, producers included the LA, private developers and a housing association, while consumers included existing households, new households and displaced households. By identifying each group in this way, and recording the relevant cost and/or benefit items accruing to them, the distributional impact of a scheme is shown very clearly. This is true not only in the case of the real costs and benefits but also for transfer payments which will not be neutral if distributional questions are of importance. Such an emphasis is clearly a desirable feature of a decision-making framework at a time when there is increasing concern that renewal schemes sometimes attract new households to an area at the expense of displacing existing low-income households.

CHAPTER EIGHT

Local Authority Housing

The previous chapter dealt with the various policies that can be employed to remove slum housing. However, in the course of the discussion it was pointed out that for a policy to eliminate slum conditions successfully it will need to combine the physical process of redevelopment or improvement with financial provisions to assist low-income households. Without this assistance slums can be expected to reappear elsewhere as these households will be unable to afford good-quality housing. There are a number of ways in which this assistance can be extended to low-income households to enable them to obtain satisfactory housing. In Britain the direct provision of Local Authority (LA) housing at rents below the market level has been the major policy used in this connection.

The history of LA housing really begins in 1919 when the Housing Act of that year placed the responsibility for dealing with the housing needs of their areas with the LAs. It was the First World War and the aspirations of the majority of the population who had lived through it that galvanised the government into action, although the need for some policy initiative had been apparent for some time. The massive rate of population growth in the nineteenth century (between 1801 and 1901 the population rose from under 9 millions to over 32 millions), together with rapid and extensive urbanisation, had produced health problems of a kind, and on a scale, not previously encountered. Public health legislation had sought to tackle some of the major problems, for example cholera, typhoid and other communicable diseases resulting from insanitary conditions, by specifying minimum housing standards, but these had inevitably involved cost increases which placed the accommodation beyond the budgets of many working-class households. Thus the need for some additional policy to enable the realisation of the original health objective became clear. The strategy adopted was the public provision of subsidised housing for the 'working classes'.[1]

Since its beginnings the fortunes of public sector housing have to a large extent been dependent upon the prevailing political climate. Sometimes this has been favourable, at other times hostile.[2] Even today, when LA housing represents over 30 per cent of the housing stock, its function and the way it discharges this function is still the centre of widespread political debate. In particular, two issues have attracted extensive attention in recent years: the first of these is how should an LA determine its rent levels, and the second is should it sell council houses to tenants who may wish to become owner-occupiers? We shall look at each of these questions in turn. But before doing so we shall consider the more fundamental issue concerning the decision to provide assistance to tenants through price subsidies rather than through a policy of general income supplementation.

Council Housing: Price Subsidies *v* Income Supplements

An LA provides housing for tenants at rents below the market level. Hence, as well as acting as a direct supplier of housing services it is also operating a policy of price (or rent) subsidisation. The form of this policy is, however, rather different from a straightforward price subsidy because it includes a quantity constraint which specifies the amount of housing a family will receive at the specified rent. The welfare implications of these dual conditions can be expressed in terms of conventional indifference curve analysis, as shown in Figure 8.1.

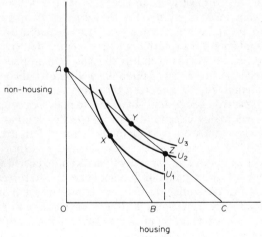

Figure 8.1 Local Authority housing: subsidies and consumption

Following the normal assumptions of this type of analysis, the rational individual in a free market can be expected to maximise his utility by selecting the combination of housing and non-housing goods indicated by point X on his budget constraint AB. The provision of LA housing at subsidised rents will reduce the price of of housing *vis-à-vis* the non-housing commodity so that the individual's budget constraint will shift outwards from *AB* to *AC*. Now if the individual was free to allocate his income in a manner of his choosing, we would expect him to select the combination of goods represented by point *Y*. However, a feature of LA housing is that typically the individual is not free to choose the quantity of housing he wishes to consume: he is allocated a house on the basis of the LA's assessment of his requirements. This will mean that there will be only one quantity of housing available to him at the subsidised price. This is shown by a second point, *Z*, on the budget constraint *AC*. Point *Z* is shown to be different to point *Y* on the assumption that the LA's assessment of the individual's housing needs is extremely unlikely to correspond exactly to the amount he would like to consume at the subsidised price. Furthermore, in this case it is assumed that the LA provides rather more housing than the individual would choose freely: this is consistent with the view sometimes heard that, given the standards prevailing in the private sector, LA 'Parker-Morris' building standards are too high (this claim is considered further below).

Critics of this form of assistance argue that the individual could reach a higher level of utility, for the same level of government expenditure, if the housing rent subsidy was replaced by a general income supplement. Furthermore, they claim that a quantity-constrained rent subsidy is even less efficient than an unconstrained one. The first assertion is based upon the well-known theorem which states that an individual will prefer a general increase in income which he is free to spend on goods of his choosing, to one of an equal amount that is related to his expenditure on a specific commodity. This proposition is demonstrated formally in Figure 8.2. In the diagram, points *X* and *Y* correspond to the pre- and post-price subsidy combinations of goods that the individual can be expected to choose. Clearly point *Y* is on a higher indifference curve and so corresponds to a greater level of consumer satisfaction. However, the individual at point *X* could also reach point *Y* if he is provided with an income supplement (prices remaining unchanged) instead of a price subsidy. The broken budget line *A'B'* passing through point *Y* indicates this possibility. (Note that the size of the subsidy is the same whether it is provided through income or through a price subsidy, that is, *AA'* when measured in terms of the non-housing good at pre-subsidy prices.) But because *A'B'* intersects U_3 at *Y* there must be a point of tangency with a higher indifference curve. This is shown as point *W* on U_4. Thus, it is argued, an income supplement will permit an individual to reach a higher level of utility than a price subsidy. Accordingly we may predict that a policy which provides cash assistance to individuals, and thereby enables them to rent housing (if they so choose)

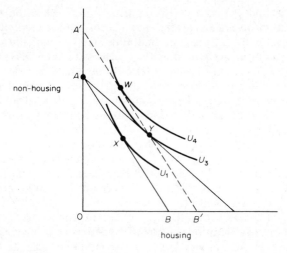

Figure 8.2   Price subsidies and income supplements

from either private or public sector suppliers charging market prices, would be preferred to one that subsidises rents.

There are, however, at least two strong counter-arguments that can be made against this claim. First, it can be argued that the foregoing analysis ignores the preferences of those individuals who provide the revenue for the subsidies. It may be that they prefer to see assistance linked to a particular 'merit' good such as housing rather than being given in the form of general cash payments which may be used to purchase commodities to which the donors attach a low priority.[3] If this is the case, any losses in potential welfare suffered by the recipients of a price subsidy may be offset by gains in welfare accruing to taxpayers. Second, the analysis assumes that an income supplement will represent an increase in real income. However, in cases where the supply of a commodity is inelastic, attempts on the part of consumers to purchase more of it with their additional money incomes may simply result in its price being bid up without producing any substantial change in the quantity available. If this happens, the budget constraint $A'B'$ in Figure 8.2 would move back towards the origin and could even (in the case of totally inelastic supply) pass through point X once again – although on this occasion it would have a steeper slope reflecting the increase in the relative price of housing. Hence, as the short-run supply of housing is known to be inelastic there is reason to doubt the claim that an income subsidy would benefit a consumer more than a price subsidy.[4]

The second criticism of LA housing policy – that the quantity constraint involves a loss of efficiency – seems to have more substance. Certainly Figure 8.1 suggests that, although the individual is in a better position with LA housing than without it (that is, Z is preferred to X), he would be in an even better position if he were able to adjust his consumption to the level of his choosing; that is, to point Y. In the example he is shown to be consuming more than he would ideally choose to do at the prevailing price ratio, a state of affairs which, as we have pointed out, some people argue exists in the LA sector because standards are set too high. But it should, of course, always be borne in mind that this result rests upon the acceptance of the sovereignty of individual preferences. In some cases we may wish to override these. For example, the incidence of externalities may mean that the individual will not choose the socially optimal quantity of housing. Similarly, the preferences of current tenants may not reflect those of future generations of tenants. This consideration is especially important in the case of a durable commodity such as housing because decisions made today will to a large extent govern the standard of housing provided for many years into the future. If, as seems likely, the increased affluence of future generations will lead them to demand a higher standard of accommodation than is generally demanded at the present time, then the LA, as the custodian of their interests, will need to take their preferences into account. More fundamentally, housing legislators may simply feel that they have a responsibility to provide accommodation of a given standard even if this does not seem to correspond to the tenant's immediate preferences. This view may be adopted because of the existence of consumer ignorance as generally understood by the economist, but it is more likely to be the expression of an attitude that does not always assign sovereignty to individuals' preferences. While such a view is rarely given pride of place by economists (with the exception of merit goods) it is worth noting that without it much of the social legislation of the past hundred years would not have been introduced.[5]

Whatever the merits and demerits of the provision of LA housing at subsidised rents, the policy has obviously become an established part of the British housing scene. Given this fact, attention often turns to the question of how the policy is operated, and, in particular, how are LA rents determined?

Finance and Rents

In the LA housing sector the pattern of rent charges and subsidies has grown up through a process which is best described as one of 'disjointed incrementalism'. Successive policies have revised, amended, modified or replaced preceding ones in a manner that has resulted in an exceedingly complicated system with no clear underlying rationale. In essence, the present system works as follows: each LA has a statutory obligation to keep a separate Housing Revenue Account which records all the costs and revenues associated with the provision of subsidised housing. The main cost items in this account are the loan charges incurred on money borrowed to finance building programmes, supervision and management expenses, and contributions towards housing repairs. Of these, loan charges are by far the most important category accounting for, on average, over 70 per cent of total costs. To meet these costs each authority receives a certain amount in subsidies from the central government. The formulae used for allocating these subsidies have been changed numerous times. At present (1978). they are related to the actual level of housing expenditure incurred by each LA, with special assistance provided for more expensive new building and in areas of high cost such as London. The remainder of their expenditure must be covered by rental income and, to a lesser extent, contributions from their general rate funds. LAs are free to determine the balance between rent and rate fund contributions and, as one might expect, proportions vary according to the political complexion of the council; approximately 35 per cent of LAs make no contribution at all although, nationally, rates produce around 10 per cent of this total income.

Once the aggregate rental income that needs to be raised has been determined, individual rents are usually set according to a rough average cost-pricing rule. This may be expressed as follows:

$$r = \frac{TC - S}{H},\tag{8.1}$$

where r = rent per unit of housing services, TC = total costs, S = central government and rate-fund subsidies and H = total number of units of housing services. Thus total costs are averaged across the entire dwelling stock and although individual dwelling rents will vary according to the size, quality and location of the dwelling (that is, the rent per unit service is constant but the rents paid by individual tenants will vary according to the level of services they receive) they are not related directly to the costs incurred on any particular dwelling. As the costs of construction have risen substantially in recent years it is the date of construction which is the main determinant of individual dwelling costs. Consequently, this averaging procedure tends to benefit those tenants living in recently constructed high-cost accommodation at the expense of tenants living in older property.[6]

In addition to rent differentials that reflect the quantity of services yielded by each dwelling other differentials have traditionally been based upon tenants' incomes. Prior to 1972 many LAs operated differential rent schemes which were based upon the circumstances of individual tenants.[7] Since 1972 a standard form of tenant subsidy has become mandatory on all LAs through the rent rebate scheme. Thus current pricing policies involve three distinct forms of subsidisation. First, there is the cross-subsidisation of tenants living in newer, more expensive property by tenants living in older dwellings that is implicit in the average cost pricing rule. Second, there are central government subsidies that are passed on to tenants in the form of a reduction (S/H) in the unit prices of housing services. And, third, there are rebates (financed by the central government) that are distributed to tenants on the basis of their income levels.

It is the second of the above subsidy arrangements – the central government to LA subsidy – that has attracted a good deal of attention in recent years and has been the subject of numerous suggestions for reform. The inflationary conditions of the 1970s have added special impetus to these calls for change, as cost increases such as those resulting from the rise in interest rates payable by LAs from under 6 per cent in 1967/8 to nearly 10 per cent in 1975/6 have resulted in substantial increases in (cost-related) central government subsidy payments. A corollary of this has been a fall in the proportion of costs covered by rent payments from nearly 77 per cent (before rebates) in 1972/3 to only 57 per cent in 1975/6.[8] One of the 1978 Labour government's responses to this situation has been to propose modifications to the subsidy allocation procedures which would increase the local contribution (rent plus rates) wherever possible, although they suggest that the fixing of individual rents should remain a matter for local discretion.[9] Thus the principles on which the allocation of the block subsidy within each LA area are to take place are left unspecified. A possible course for policy initiative in this direction would be to treat separately the LA's function as a pricer of housing services from its function as an allocator of subsidies. At present these roles are combined, with the result that the different principles governing each activity become obscured.

As far as the first function is concerned – that is, the pricing of housing services – probably the most widely advocated pricing rule for a public sector operator is that of marginal cost pricing. By setting a price equal to the marginal costs of production it can be shown that, given certain assumptions, the social surplus (that is, consumers' plus producers' surplus) resulting from the production and consumption of the relevant commodity will be maximised.[10] In the case of housing, increments in the supply of services are provided through new building, and, as we have seen already, increases in costs through time have resulted in significantly higher costs being incurred on recently built housing than that incurred on housing built some time ago. This means that the marginal cost schedule for the supply of LA housing services will be low and flat for most of its range (corresponding to those services provided by low-cost, older housing), but will rise sharply as the limits of the existing stock are reached. (See Figure 8.3.)

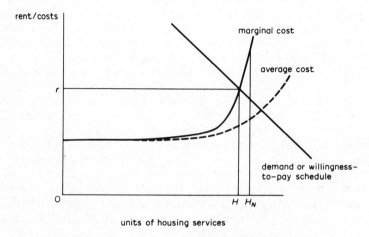

Figure 8.3 Marginal cost pricing and LA housing

Application of the marginal cost pricing rule requires that rents should be set equal to the cost of producing the marginal unit of housing services. If a conventional demand schedule exists both the rent, r, and the quantity of housing services, $0H$, will be determined simultaneously as in Figure 8.3, at the point of equality between demand and marginal cost. In the case of LA housing, however, normal demand conditions do not apply; nevertheless prospective and existing tenants can be expected to have a 'willingness-to-pay' schedule which, if identifiable, would perform the same function.[11] Alternatively, an LA may specify a quantity of housing to be provided, such as $0H_N$, according to its assessment of need and resources; this would similarly determine a marginal cost figure but would not, according to the classical postulates of consumer sovereignty, necessarily produce the optimal output. In each scheme, however, the rule would involve charging a rent for the entire housing stock which is related to the costs of providing new housing. (Note that this does not mean that the rent of old and new housing will be identical, because it is the *price per unit* of housing services that is uniform; as long as new housing offers a greater quantity of services it will command a higher rent.)

Relating all rents to the costs of providing new housing in this way is bound to encounter opposition from the mass of existing tenants living in older housing who, because of their length of residence, are unlikely to consider themselves marginal users in the way that a user of a currently produced non-durable commodity may be willing to do. As such they would be unlikely to see the justification for their meeting current marginal costs, especially as this would produce substantial profits for the LA.[12] But the pricing arrangement would be only the first part of the LA's housing policy. In addition, there would be a second part dealing with subsidies. Hence if it were decided that tenants merited preferential treatment according to their length of residence, this basically distributional issue could be dealt with alongside other criteria, such as household income, family size etc., which would be used to determine eligibility for subsidisation. In fact, the 1972 Housing Act attempted to distinguish the principles governing pricing from those governing the allocation of subsidies by extending the concept of a 'fair rent' (see Chapter Six) to the LA housing sector, while offering rent allowances to low-income tenants. However, the politically partial nature of this Act (there was no attempt to reform the financial arrangements covering owner-occupiers, revenue for subsidies was intended to come primarily from the rents of other council tenants rather than from the population at large, etc.) meant that it attracted vigorous political opposition which led to its eventual repeal.

Even if the particular objections encountered by the 1972 Act were avoided, it must be conceded that most attempts to deal with subsidisation separately will encounter the objections that are invariably levied against selective as opposed to universal welfare schemes. These are, notably, that they reduce the rate of take-up of subsidies because eligible claimants are either not aware of their eligibility, or, for reasons of pride or whatever, are unwilling to identify themselves. Others will object because they prefer the more collectivist principles incorporated in current LA average cost pricing practices.[13] Considerations of this latter type are, of course, of fundamental importance in dealing with our next topic; that is, the sale of council houses.

Council House Sales

Without doubt the major determinant of a person's attitude towards council house sales is his ideological position: does he prefer a system in which property in general, or residential property in particular, is owned privately or does he prefer public ownership? Ultimately, of course, this is a matter of personal value judgement and as such economic analysis does not have much to contribute towards it. On the other hand, however, there are a number of considerations concerning the effects of council house sales which rest upon statements of a positive nature and these are amenable to economic analysis. In particular, there is the question of whether an LA gains financially through the sale of its housing and thereby increases the funds at its disposal. Let us examine the basis on which such claims are usually made.

At its most simple level, such a claim may involve a comparison between the sum an LA receives for the sale of a house (usually the notional market price less a discount of up to 20 per cent which is offered to existing tenants) with the sum of the outstanding debt. Not surprisingly this will almost inevitably suggest that a substantial 'profit' will be realised through a sale, particularly in the case of older property which was built when costs were considerably lower than at present. Clearly, however, this is a fallacious result because the historic cost of a durable commodity such as housing (to which the outstanding debt relates) is irrelevant as far as its present-day value is concerned. The current value of the asset is reflected in its market value and it is this sum which should be compared with the sum the LA actually receives. On this basis a sale at a discount below the market price would appear to involve a capital loss. However, this may not be the case, as we shall see below.

A rather more sophisticated procedure involves considering the time profile of costs and revenues associated with a council house over the duration of its remaining life to see whether the present discounted value (PDV) of future net returns is greater (or less) than the sum that would be realised through a sale. This procedure would be unnecessary if there was a perfect market in housing and other capital assets because the PDV of future net returns would be equal to the capital value of the house (see Chapter One), but clearly the conditions of a perfect market do not apply to the LA housing sector, where, as we have seen, rents are administered below the market level. Accordingly, calculations that aim to identify and evaluate the PDVs of the various housing cost and revenue items shown in Table 8.1 are often carried out.

The gains to be realised through a sale are largely self-explanatory: they include the sale price and the management, maintenance and interest expenses that are avoided once the LA ceases to own the property. The losses include the rental income forgone, the value of

TABLE 8.1

Revenue and cost items relevant to council house sales (all expressed in PDVs)

Gains through sale
(1) Sale price
(ii) Reduced management expenses
(iii) Reduced maintenance and repair expenditures
(iv) Reduced interest charges

Losses through sale
(i) Rental income
(ii) Terminal value of the site
(iii) Government subsidies

---

the site at the end of the life of the property and the subsidy per year payable to the LA from the central government which is related to the annual costs incurred on the property. In a recent article, Murie (1977) has scrutinised some of the figures relating to council house sales released by Leeds City Council. He concludes that there would be an average capitalised net loss of nearly £8000 resulting from the sale of a modern council house (one with a remaining life of fifty-six years). This conclusion is in stark contrast to the Council's claim that a net gain of £1225 would be realised through the sale of such a house. The different predictions arise because of varying assumptions about the relative growth rates of LA housing expenses (that is, management and maintenance and repair expenditure) and rental income which, given the time horizon of over fifty years, are clearly crucial to the final result. Without becoming involved in the details of this debate, we can none the less say that the greater the rate of growth of rental income and the lower the rate of growth of expenditure, the less advantageous a policy involving sales will become to an LA. If a sale does take place, but the demand for housing services rises so that the additional rental income would have been greater than the additional costs, the benefit that would have accrued to the LA will now accrue to the private owner in the form of house price appreciation.

CHAPTER NINE

Taxation and Subsidies

In the preceding chapters we have seen how various policies assist different tenure groups within the housing market. For example, rent control reduces the rent that the private tenant has to pay below its free market level; tax relief on mortgage interest payments increases the disposable income of many home owners; and LA charging practices result in lower rents for council tenants than would prevail in a free market. Not surprisingly, one of the most persistent debates surrounding this area of government activity concerns the overall distributional consequences of these policies. Specifically, what are the relative benefits accruing to owner-occupiers, private tenants and LA tenants as a result of the combined effect of these taxes and subsidies? And to what extent can the pattern of assistance be considered equitable?

In this chapter an attempt is made to assemble the information necessary to answer these questions. But a word of warning is in order at the outset. This is an extremely complex area in which unequivocal judgements are difficult (some would say impossible) to reach. This is partly because questions of distribution and equity inevitably involve normative judgements; but it is also because, at a less general level, there is often disagreement about what should actually be measured for purposes of comparison between groups. The search for a generally acceptable definition of a 'subsidy' is a good illustration of this dilemma.[1] Indeed, problems associated with this and other bases for comparison led the authors of the recent Government Housing Policy Review to dismiss much of the debate about equity between tenure groups as 'sterile' because, they maintain, it involves comparing 'chalk and cheese'.[2] But a total rejection of all inter-group comparisons would be too severe a reaction. Various qualified judgements are certainly possible. In fact, the Review itself has made a major contribution to this task by assembling the most comprehensive collection of conceptual arguments and data yet to appear on the subject. The remainder of this chapter makes extensive use of this material.

Concepts and the Measurement of Subsidies

We shall conduct our examination by looking at the treatment of the three main tenure groups as this is the basis on which most of the debate concerning housing finance has been conducted. However, as we shall see in the final section, consideration of the equity of housing policy may be better served by a tenure-free analysis which concentrates on the treatment of different *income* groups. But this is to look ahead. Before we reach this point a number of conceptual issues need to be resolved so that analysis of the empirical information can proceed. The first of these is the general one applicable to all tenure groups to which we have referred already; that is, how do we define a 'subsidy'? Of the many alternatives, possibly the most useful procedure is to use the term to refer to any aspect of government policy that results in a household bearing less than the full costs of their housing. This definition has the advantage of a generality that will enable us to include the effects of a diverse set of policies. For example, it will include rent control, which certainly assists many households but does not actually involve public expenditure, and income-tax relief, which renders benefits through the non-collection of taxes that otherwise would be due, as well as more conventional subsidy payments. The remaining conceptual problems concern the treatment of subsidies made to particular tenure groups and so we shall deal with each of these groups in turn before moving on to consider the empirical evidence.

Owner-Occupiers

As we have seen already, few households are in a position to buy a house outright from their current income and accumulated savings. Most people require a long-term loan before they can become home owners. However, once a mortgage loan has been obtained the borrower may − under present tax arrangements − deduct the interest payments he makes from his gross income to determine the amount of income that is liable to taxation. Or to describe the practice somewhat differently, income earned to pay mortgage interest charges is exempt from taxation. There is an upper limit to the amount of tax relief that can be obtained in this way (at present it is only available on loans of up to £25 000), but given the importance of interest payments (which in the early years of a loan represent the bulk of annual payments), this represents a substantial supplement to the incomes of mortgage holders. It is, of course, this tax relief which is conventionally identified as the subsidy accruing to home owners. However, it can be argued that this is not really an appropriate measure of the subsidy payment for purposes of comparison between owner-occupiers and other tenure groups, because the same subsidy is available to private landlords who can also deduct interest charges as a cost of production when calculating their taxable profits, and pass the benefit on to their tenants (see below). Tax payments made on rental income, on the other hand, are treated differently in the two sectors and for this reason they provide a better basis for comparison. The inconsistency of treatment can be best understood by considering the respective roles of the owner-occupier and the private landlord.

Conceptually, the owner-occupier can be looked upon as both a consumer and a holder of an asset which supplies housing services. That he is a consumer is fairly obvious, but what is less apparent is that because he owns his house (or at least an equity share in it) he is providing housing services in the same way as a private landlord. Unlike the private landlord, however, both the owner and the tenant roles are vested in one individual: he is supplying services to himself. It is because of this synthesis of roles that the owner-occupier avoids a tax burden that falls on the private landlord and/or his tenant; that is, the private landlord pays tax on the income he receives from supplying housing services (the burden of which will be distributed between himself and his tenant according to the elasticities of demand and supply in the private rented sector) whereas the owner-occupier does not. Of course, the income of the former is real and arises through a market transaction whereas the latter's is only imputed but, nevertheless, the absence of taxation on owner-occupiers means that the cost to them of consuming a given quantity of housing services is lower than it is in the private rented sector where some expenditure is diverted to the government. The relative advantage accruing to owner-occupiers because of this tax exemption has been clarified by Rosenthal (1975), who has broken down the relative housing costs faced by the owner-occupier and the private tenant.

Using an algebraic formulation, he assumes that the gross income of the renter (Y_R) is equal to the gross income of the owner-occupier (Y_O) plus the non-pecuniary income the owner-occupier receives through his ownership of his house (iE). Thus,

$$Y_R = Y_O + iE, \qquad (9.1)$$

where i = the (for simplicity) uniform rate of return on all capital, and E = the owner-occupier's equity holding in his house.

Furthermore, if we assume that the owner-occupier and the renter live in identical houses with the same current market value (P), then the competitive rent level will be iP (ignoring complications introduced by maintenance, depreciation and running costs). Finally we may assume that a standard income tax rate (t) applies to both individuals. Now the disposable income of the renter (Y_R^D) after tax payments and housing costs will be:

$$Y_R^D = Y_R(1-t) - iP, \qquad (9.2)$$

whereas the disposable income of the owner-occupier after his tax and housing costs will be:

$$Y_O^D = Y_O(1-t) - i(P-E) + i(P-E)t, \qquad (9.3)$$

where $(P-E)$ is the amount of his mortgage, $i(P-E)$ his mortgage interest payments, and $i(P-E)t$ the tax relief on these payments.

Now by using these two measures of disposable income, we may say that the relative advantage accruing to the owner-occupier will be indicated by the excess of his after-tax, after-housing costs income. Thus subtracting equation (9.2) from equation (9.3) we obtain:

$$Y_O^D - Y_R^D = (Y_O - Y_R)(1-t) + iE(1-t) + tiP, \qquad (9.4)$$

but from equation (9.1) we know that

$$Y_O - Y_R = -iE$$

$$\therefore Y_O^D - Y_R^D = tiP. \qquad (9.5)$$

Thus the advantage received by the owner-occupier is shown to be equal to the tax relief on the imputed income obtained from the property rather than the tax relief received on the mortgage interest payments. Moreover, note that this subsidy is related to the current market value of the house and will therefore increase with its value even though the mortgage payments — which will be related to its value at the time of acquisition — and the tax relief associated with them will remain constant.[3]

In fact this subsidy has not always been available to home owners. Until 1963 they were liable to Schedule A taxation on the imputed income they received from their property. This meant that, in principle, the owner-occupier was treated in the same manner as the private landlord: he was taxed on his income and able to set the cost of capital against his taxes. However, in practice, the infrequent updating of property valuations meant that home owners were seriously undertaxed and as a result the revenue collected from this source was very small. In consequence the tax was removed in that year and this has produced the present inconsistency of treatment.

The second major subsidy item that is usually accredited to the home owner is the exemption from capital gains taxation of property used for owner-occupation. Once again there is a contrast between the position of the private landlord/tenant and the owner-occupier in that the former is liable to this tax whereas the latter is not. One argument that is often put forward against a capital gains tax on owner-occupied property is that house price appreciation does not lead to any real gains for the owner because he is unable to realise the gain without selling his property and, even if he does sell it, he will need to allocate the same amount to buy a comparable quantity of housing elsewhere. But both of these propositions neglect important sources of gain that do accrue to the owner-occupier through capital appreciation. On the first point, there are now a number of financial institutions that are willing to offer loans against the collateral of property that has appreciated beyond the owner's original mortgage commitment. This provides the owner-occupier with access to credit which enables him to allocate his expenditure through time in a way that reliance upon current income would not permit him to do. In this way even unrealised capital gains yield a benefit to the asset owner. As far as the second point is concerned, it is true that if all property increases in value at the same rate there is no scope for increased housing consumption if the household's consumption of other commodities remains unchanged. However, the change in relative prices, and the associated increase in the value of the owner-occupier's real balances, does offer him the opportunity of substituting relatively less expensive non-housing goods for the now more expensive housing and thereby reaching a preferred welfare position.[4] And so once again the scope for a gain does indeed exist.

Ultimately one's attitude towards the absence of capital gains taxation, and indeed to the absence of taxes on imputed income, will depend on whether house purchase for owner-occupation is viewed as a consumption or an investment activity. If it is viewed as consumption, it can be argued that these taxes are no more appropriate than they are in the case of other consumer durables, such as cars and televisions, where there are also both rental- and owner-user markets but no proposals for taxing imputed incomes and capital gains.[5] On the other hand, the investment aspect of housing (putting one's money into 'bricks and mortar') does seem to figure quite prominently in determining many people's housing expenditures and, to this extent, it would seem legitimate to view it as at least partly an investment activity that should be subject to the normal taxation practices.

Finally, even if one does accept that these tax exemptions do constitute subsidies to owner-occupiers, some observers have argued that their impact upon house prices has been such that little benefit has finally accrued to the original recipients. This argument maintains that the subsidies to owner-occupiers have, by increasing their disposable incomes, raised the bid prices they have been willing to offer for housing. In a market where there is inelastic supply this has resulted in higher prices and a transfer of benefits to the owners of the fixed factor, that is, landowners. The importance of this argument obviously depends upon the price elasticity of housing supply which, as we have seen, there is good reason to suppose is rather inelastic, although opinions on this matter vary.[6]

Local Authority Tenants

We saw in Chapter Eight that LAs receive housing subsidies from the government which many of them augment with local contributions from their general rate funds, and that together these payments enable them to set rents below the level that otherwise would be necessary to balance their housing revenue accounts. In addition, individual LA tenants are able to claim rent rebates if their incomes are deemed insufficient to meet their rent commitments given their family and other circumstances. When assessing the amount of subsidy received by LA tenants, it is the normal procedure to base the calculations on these general and rent rebate subsidies. So, for example, figures indicating the total subsidy going to LA tenants or the average subsidy per tenant are often produced. (The empirical section of this chapter does, in fact, contain such estimates.) However, just as the readily identifiable measure of tax relief on interest payments may not be the appropriate one to use in the case of the owner-occupier, so it can be argued that the conventionally used cash payment figures are an erroneous measure of the true subsidies accruing to LA tenants.

To illustrate this point, it will be recalled that in calculating its total housing costs an LA records the loan charges it actually incurs on the different vintages of housing it owns. That is, its accounting procedures are based on 'historic' costs. However, as the price of housing has risen substantially through time, it has been argued that this leads to a serious underestimation of the opportunity costs of older LA housing. As a durable good in a market where the existing stock is large in relation to currently produced housing, older housing will have a current value that is demand- rather than cost-determined. In so far as costs are relevant, it will be the costs of new housing rather than historic costs which are relevant in the determination of value (assuming, of course, that old and new housing are substitutable). Arguments of this type have led Rosenthal (1977) to define the subsidy received by an LA tenant as the difference between the rent he actually pays and the rent that would be payable if the same housing were available on the private market.

There are, however, substantial practical difficulties associated with the use of such a measure. In particular, the estimation of hypothetical free market rents is likely to pose special problems. The normal procedure is to base these estimates on the prices of comparable owner-occupied housing on the assumptions that these are determined in a free market. But we have seen already that government taxation policies in the owner-occupied sector are likely to have influenced demand and price levels there (unless supply is perfectly elastic), and so these prices would need to be 'purged' of any policy-induced component before they could be used as a benchmark. Moreover, if the sizeable (non-marginal) stock of LA housing was, in reality, added to the private stock the general effects on supply and demand would without doubt be sufficiently pronounced to establish a quite different set of prices to those prevailing in the private sector at the moment. Nevertheless the principles underlying this method of calculating subsidies are clear and so despite these problems we shall consider the results obtained when using them in our section on empirical evidence.

Private Tenants

If the conventional view of a subsidy as a cash payment is adopted the position of the private tenant is rather different from that of the owner-occupier or LA tenant. For although private tenants are eligible for selective assistance through rent allowances in the same way that LA tenants are eligible for rent rebates, the rate of take-up of these allowances is very low. By far the most important form of assistance they receive comes to them through the price controls imposed by the government on private landlords. As we saw in Chapter Six, numerous rent-control policies, and latterly rent regulation, have acted to keep rents below the levels they would reach in a free or unregulated market. Now while this form of assistance does not correspond to the generally used definition of a subsidy (not least because it is financed by the landlord rather than the government), it is in fact, precisely the measure which Rosenthal argues is the true subsidy in the case of LA housing, that is, the difference between the rent actually paid and the free market rent. As such, however, the same reservations must apply concerning the possibility of actually estimating the size of this subsidy.

Distribution Between Tenure Groups: Empirical Evidence

The previous three sections have raised some of the conceptual problems surrounding the measurement of subsidies. In so doing, each section has outlined the way in which subsidies allocated to the three main tenure groups are usually calculated, and then gone on to argue that there are alternative measures which are theoretically more sound. In this section we shall continue to use this approach. First, we shall present some empirical information on the distribution of subsidies as conventionally understood and then we shall give some rough indication of how the picture changes if the alternative measures are used. The latter set of figures will necessarily be subject to far greater errors of estimation but in their defence we may quote the view of E. J. Mishan, who argues that 'there is more to be said for rough estimates of the precise concept than precise estimates of economically irrelevant concepts'. (Mishan, 1971*b*).

The Government's Housing Policy Review lists a number of alternative ways in which the distribution of subsidies between tenure groups may be expressed.[7] It does, however, confine its comparisons to the two major groups, owner-occupiers and LA tenants, on the grounds that private tenants receive little in the form of cash assistance whereas the complexity of the rent regulation system makes it well-nigh impossible to obtain an accurate measure of the average effect of rent control. Unfortunately, therefore, in the absence of any better information our comparisons are similarly restricted to two groups, although we shall return to consider the position of private tenants in our discussion of the equity of housing finance. As far as owner-occupiers and LA tenants are concerned, probably the two most widely-quoted subsidy measures are the total amounts received by each tenure group and the average subsidy received per household in each group. Table 9.1 gives this information for two selected years: 1972/73, which was the first year in which rent rebates were offered, and 1975/76, which is the latest year for which figures are available.

From the table it can be seen that in 1975/6 the average annual subsidy per LA tenant was £214 if rent rebate payments were included and £173 if they were not. (Whether or not rent rebates should be considered as housing subsidies has been a subject of debate. Some commentators claim that because they are related to income, they should be regarded as part of the government's general welfare policy instead of a housing measure. Others point out that they are specifically related to housing expenditure and that, furthermore, they are not available to owner-occupiers and so cannot be described as part of a *general* income maintenance policy.) Compared with the subsidies received by LA tenants, the average tax relief/option mortgage subsidy received by the owner-occupier was somewhat lower.[8] This worked out at £96 per year if the total subsidy bill was averaged over the entire owner-occupier population, or at £174 per year if it was measured only in terms of those owner-occupiers

TABLE 9.1
Subsidies and tax relief by tenure group (United Kingdom)

Local Authority tenants	1972/3	1975/6
Number of tenants (thousands)	5 840	6 180
Exchequer subsidies and rate fund contributions (£ million)	324	1 066
Rent rebates (£ million)	77	256
Average subsidy per tenant excluding rent rebates (£ per year)	56	173
Average subsidy per tenant including rent rebates (£ per year)	69	214

Owner-Occupiers		
Number of owner-occupiers (thousands)	9 350	10 000
Number of owner-occupiers with mortgage loans (thousands)	5 142*	5 500
Tax relief and option mortgage subsidies (£ million)	391	957
Average relief/option mortgage subsidy per owner-occupier (£ per year)	42	96
Average relief/option mortgage subsidy per mortgagee (£ per year)	76	174

* Estimate based on 1975/6.
Source: *Housing Policy* (H.M.S.O., 1977), *Technical Volume*, part ii, table vi, p. 19.

actually receiving a subsidy (that is, those home owners with mortgage loans). In both cases, however, the figures indicate that the average LA tenant received a rather larger subsidy than the average owner-occupier. Moreover, a glance at the corresponding figures for 1972/3 shows that the differential has widened in recent years.

A similar result is obtained if the alternative definitions of owner-occupier and LA tenant subsidies discussed in the earlier part of this chapter are used. The amount of subsidy received by LA tenants in terms of the difference between actual and notional market rents has been estimated by Rosenthal (1977). To do this he requires an estimate of the notional rent, which he obtains in the following manner. First, he estimates the relationship between the purchase price of recently traded owner-occupied housing and its rateable value; second, using this relationship, he predicts the notional market price of LA housing on the basis of its rateable value. Finally, by assuming a gross real rate of return on property of 8 per cent per annum, he computes the rent that a private landlord would require to produce this return (that is, he uses the relationship $r = iP$, explained in Chapter One). Unfortunately, his figures relate to 1969, and to England and Wales rather than the entire United Kingdom, and so they are not directly comparable with those given in Table 9.1. But they do suggest that subsidy payments calculated on this basis are substantially higher than those obtained through the conventional procedure. He suggests that the subsidy per dwelling in 1969 was approximately £144 compared with the official figure of about £35.

For purposes of comparison, we have carried out some simple calculations to gain some idea of the relative size of owner-occupier subsidies for the same year when looked at in terms of the absence of taxes on imputed income. Using the average dwelling price for that year as indicated by the building societies' returns to the Ministry of Housing and Local Government, and the gross rate of return figure of 8 per cent used above, an estimate of owner-occupiers' imputed income has been obtained. Then the standard marginal rate of taxation has been applied to this income to calculate the tax subsidy. This produces a figure of £92 per owner-occupier which is substantially above the conventional tax-relief figure for 1969 of £28. It is, however, still below the LA tenant subsidy figure, although it is not clear how far this is the result of the undoubted negative bias involved in this simple computational procedure.[9] Moreover, it should be borne in mind that no account has been taken of the lack of capital gains tax. Hence it would seem prudent to avoid strong statements about the distribution of subsidies if they are based on these latter definitions.

So far we have been preoccupied with the amounts of subsidy received by households in the different tenure groups as this is often considered to be the basic issue as far as the equity of housing subsidies is concerned. However, as we pointed out at the beginning of this chapter, judgements about the equity of consumer subsidies may be better served by taking account of the relative income levels of the recipients rather than by just looking at their tenure categories.

Income Distribution, Subsidies and Equity

Table 9.2 shows the distribution of household income and mean income levels for the three main tenure groups as estimated by the *Family Expenditure Survey* for 1975.

A number of important points are revealed in Table 9.2. First, it shows the heavy concentration of low-income earners in the private

TABLE 9.2
Household income by tenure group, 1975

£ pa	LA	Private rented (unfurnished)	Percentage O/occupier (with mortgages)	O/occupier (total)
Under 1 000	13	20	1	7
1 000–1 499	13	16	1	7
1 500–1 999	7	11	2	6
2 000–2 999	17	16	12	14
3 000–3 999	19	15	22	18
4 000–4 999	13	11	23	18
5 000 and over	18	11	39	30
	100	100	100	100
Mean household income (£ pa)	3 214	2 697	4 916	4 241

Source: *Family Expenditure Survey*, 1975.

rented sector: nearly 50 per cent of these households earned less than £2 000 per year. These earnings figures, together with those of the *Housing Condition Surveys* discussed in Chapters Two and Six. confirm that this sector contains widespread poverty and housing stress, and yet only a small amount of direct cash subsidies are allocated to this sector.[10] At the other end of the spectrum the extent of relative prosperity in the owner-occupied sector is indicated by the incidence of higher income groups there. Especially this is true among households with mortgage loans, where over 60 per cent have incomes of over £4 000 p.a. Finally, in assessing the equity of the average subsidies received by owner-occupiers and LA tenants, it is clearly of relevance to note that the average owner-occupier (with a loan) has an income that is over 50 per cent higher than the average LA tenant's income.

These, however, are only mean figures, and the table shows that there is considerable dispersion around the mean. It is therefore of interest to know how the subsidies are distributed between the various income groups within each tenure category. Table 9.3 provides this information.

The amounts of tax relief accruing to owner-occupiers are based upon FES returns which record household mortgage interest payments and incomes (and hence eligibility for tax relief). It is known

138   *Aspects of Policy*

TABLE 9.3
*Tax relief, subsidies and income distribution,
England Wales, 1974/5 (£ pa)* *

Income of head of household and wife	Owner-occupiers: average tax relief or option mortgage subsidy	LA tenants' subsidy
Under 1000	59	168
1000–1499	73	168
1500–1999	91	159
2000–2499	104	160
2500–2999	101	137
3000–3499	129	147
3500–3999	129	154
4000–4999	148	164
5000–5999	179 ⎱	154
Over 6000	369 ⎰	

* As these figures refer to the financial year 1974/5 and only to England and
Wales, they are not directly comparable with the figures in either Table 9.1
or Table 9.2.
Source: *Housing Policy* (H.M.S.O., 1977), *Technical Volume* I, table IV. 36
and IV. 37, pp. 213–14.

that the FES under-records mortgage interest payments and there
are reasons for suspecting that this and other factors may result in a
relative understatement of the benefits accuring to higher income
groups.[11] Even so the figures indicate a sharp increase in the average
tax relief received as income rises, although it rises less fast than
income. In the case of LA tenant subsidies, we have seen that the
difficulties associated with estimating a notional free market rent have
made government officials reluctant to use such a concept. And yet a
measure of the 'unsubsidised' rent per dwelling is required if an
estimate of the subsidy received by tenants with different incomes
living in different qualities of housing is to be made. In the event, the
authors of the Housing Policy Review defined individual rents in
relation to the gross rateable value of each dwelling in such a way that
rents in total covered the aggregate historic costs of the entire housing
stock. On this basis, as Table 9.3 shows, the average subsidy does not
change much with income: this suggests that the policy is 'progressive'
in the sense that the subsidy/income ratio falls as income rises. On

these grounds we may conclude that subsidy policy operated *within* the public sector is more progressive (and equitable?) than the policy towards owner-occupiers. As far as a tenure-free analysis is concerned it is fairly certain that the average amount of assistance increases with income but less than proportionately.

Postscript

This book has attempted to demonstrate how the application of microeconomic methods of analysis can aid our understanding of the way in which the housing market operates. It has done so by indicating how particular models of market behaviour can be used to represent many of the special features of this market, and by showing how the demand for housing and the conditions under which it is supplied can be analysed. Hence, a capital stock adjustment model has been shown to be one way of representing a market in which there is a large existing stock of the commodity – resulting from its extreme durability – and substantial time lags in the response of new construction to changes in demand. Similarly, an approach based upon the identification of specific housing attributes has been shown to be a suitable method for dealing with the heterogeneity of housing and its role in determining relative prices, while the linkages between individual dwellings and sub-markets have been highlighted by a matrix formulation. On the subject of demand analysis, an attempt has been made to indicate how applied research has been carried out in this area, and to point to some of the major methodological problems that have been encountered and some of the results obtained. A similar emphasis upon applied research has been adopted in dealing with the construction industry where information on its organisation and performance has been assembled.

In addition to this examination of market behaviour, this book has also endeavoured to show how the same general methods of analysis can be used to investigate the role of the public sector within the housing market. Thus rent control has been analysed with the aid of a stock adjustment model, while the 'attributes' approach has provided a new perspective on the process of property deterioration often associated with this control. The demand and supply conditions resulting in the formation of areas of slum housing have been examined and the contribution of economic analysis towards the evaluation of policy options for the renewal of these areas have been discussed. Questions relating to the provision of LA housing – including the choice to be made between providing assistance through price or income subsidies, and the principles governing the setting of rents – were similarly shown to be amenable to economic analysis. Finally, the vexed question of the distribution of housing subsidies has been shown to benefit from the clarification of the principles involved that economic analysis can offer, even though it can by no means resolve all the disagreements present in this debate. In many ways it is this last judgement that points to the strengths and weaknesses of the approach adopted in this book. Its strength is that, it is hoped, it has provided the reader with a better understanding of the operation of the housing market than he possessed previously. And few people would dispute that information on, for example, the income elasticity of demand, or the effect of rent control on housing quality, or the relative costs of renovation and rebuilding, or any of the numerous other issues dealt with in this book, are important if policies are to be devised to achieve the housing objectives society sets itself. But – and this is its weakness – it says little about the selection of these objectives. Instead it has adopted the procedure commonly employed by economists of subsuming a diverse set of policy objectives within a single general form. Thus a cost-benefit study of an urban renewal project involving many different policy elements will typically be evaluated in terms of whether or not it leads to a potential Pareto improvement. This procedure as used by its practitioners is not designed to elucidate the process of choice between multiple objectives: in the above case prior acceptance of the individual's willingness-to-pay as the chosen indicator of social preferences precludes such an examination. Many people will argue that this approach actively obscures the crucial issue of choice between policy options. And it must be conceded that for many of the topics dealt with in this book, especially those concerning the distribution of subsidies, it is the choice of objectives that is of primary importance. A defence of the approach adopted here is to argue that this task is properly the function of the political process and not the direct concern of the economist *qua* economist. But it should be recorded that this view will not be shared by those who maintain that the selection of objectives can only be explained in terms of the prevailing dominant political and/or economic institutions – a school of thought which extends from radical Marxian analysts to 'public choice' economic theorists. To them, questions involving how and by whom objectives are selected constitute the essential subject-matter of the political economy of housing.

Notes and References

Introduction

1. Crouch and Wolf (1972) p. 26.
2. Hansard, 1974–5, vol. 881, col. 914.
3. See Wilkinson (1971*b*).
4. See the Postscript of this book for a brief discussion of the role of economics in the decision-making process.

Chapter 1

1. In this context the term rent is used to refer to the entire payment made for housing services and not in the narrower, more precise sense associated with the term 'economic rent' (that is, the income received by any factor in excess of its transfer earnings). The similarity of the terms is not, of course, coincidental, for the concept of economic rent was developed originally by Ricardo with reference to the payments made to the owners of land. See Stonier and Hague (1972) ch. 13 for a convenient summary of Ricardian theory and the development of the concept.
2. This is a specific application of a general approach to consumer theory that was formulated by Lancaster (1966). The work of a number of writers who have applied the Lancastrian concepts to the housing market is discussed in Chapter Three.
3. Turvey (1957) p. 48.
4. Competition between households is the residential component of the more general competitive process involving different land uses: commercial, industrial, recreational, etc.
5. This practice is also related to the previous discussion of cautious lending policies because building societies could vary interest rates charged to borrowers according to their assessment of the risks involved on a particular loan (as, for instance, insurance companies vary their premiums), instead of applying the more crude lend/don't lend dichotomy.

Chapter 2

1. Under the Housing Act of 1969 a dwelling may be deemed unfit for habitation if it is considered to be so far defective in one or more of the following as to be not reasonably suitable for accommodation: repair, stability, freedom from damp, internal arrangement, natural lighting, ventilation, water supply, drainage and sanitary conveniences, facilities for the preparation and cooking of food and for the disposal of waste water.

Chapter 3

1. One common form of the expectations hypothesis postulates that the currently-held expectation of the future price level may be expressed as the weighted average of the expectation held last period and the actual price observed currently. That is,

$$p_t^e = \gamma p_{t-1}^e + (1 - \gamma) P_t, \text{ where } 0 < \gamma < 1.$$

See Christ (1966) p. 206.

2. We have assumed that housing is supplied under conditions of constant long-run costs, so that the same equilibrium price P^* applies at the two different optimum stock levels. But the model could be modified quite easily to take account of either increasing or decreasing cost conditions. Suppose, for example, that housing is subject to increasing costs because of a long-run rise in the price of a factor input such as land. This may be represented by a series of upward shifts in the new construction industry supply curve through time and a long-run supply schedule with a positive slope. For a given change in demand conditions, this would result in a higher long-run equilibrium price and a somewhat lower optimum stock than was observed in the constant cost case – the exact magnitude of the difference depending upon the size of the long-run supply price elasticity.

3. An alternative matrix formulation is presented by Goodall (1972). He uses it to represent the entire housing stock within a given area instead of just that portion which is considered to be 'for sale'. (Formally the distinction between dwellings for sale and others is a dubious one, for, presumably, most dwellings are for sale at some price. However, the distinction is usually employed to distinguish between owners who have extraneous reasons for wishing to move, for example because of a change of workplace, and those who do not. In the latter case, it is probable that owners do not anticipate that they would find a buyer with a ceiling price above their floor price and, therefore, they do not bother to take the active steps necessary to inform buyers of their floor price. This effectively removes their property from the market.) He further assumes that if an area is self-contained each buyer will need to vacate a house and is, therefore, also a prospective seller. Within this framework, the failure of a transaction to take place may simply be a reflection of the equilibrium of those households who do not wish to move.

4. Other writers who have used the matrix method with specific reference to filtering include Smith (1972) and Edel (1972).

5. Heilbrun (1974) p. 251.

6. Some other writers – notably Fisher and Winnick (1951) and Lowry (1960) – define filtering simply in terms of relative price changes. Neither of them consider a change in occupancy to be a necessary part of the process, although it may well be a consequence of it. However, as Grigsby points out, this definition may facilitate greater precision in certain types of empirical work, but it strips the concept of much of its intrinsic interest. For it is the change in user that distinguishes filtering from the more ordinary process of durable price depreciation.

7. Chapter One contains a discussion of how transactions costs and imperfect information act as impediments to movement and can thereby produce distortions in housing consumption patterns.

8. Wilkinson describes factor analysis as 'a multivariate technique which tries to identify the underlying influences which affect the behaviour of the observed variates and the relationships among them'. (Wilkinson, 1973, p. 76.) He goes on to summarise the way it can be used to explain relative house prices in the following way:

House prices (P) may be expressed as a function of n latent factors (F) so that:

$$P = f(F_1, F_2, F_3, \ldots, F_n), \tag{1}$$

where each F is a linear combination of m variables

$$F = \sum_1^m a_i x_i \qquad m > n \tag{2}$$

($x_1, x_2, \ldots, x_m$ are the observed variables, e.g. plot size, number of rooms, number of bedrooms, etc., and $a_1, a_2, \ldots, a_m$ represent the factor 'loadings' associated with each variable and its factor.)

The statistical technique of factor analysis actually provides the set of factor loadings, thus:

$$F_1 = \alpha_1 x_1 + \beta_1 x_2 + \ldots + \gamma_1 x_m$$
$$F_2 = \alpha_2 x_1 + \beta_2 x_2 + \ldots + \gamma_2 x_m$$
$$\cdot \qquad \cdot \qquad \cdot \qquad \cdot$$
$$\cdot \qquad \cdot \qquad \cdot \qquad \cdot$$
$$\cdot \qquad \cdot \qquad \cdot \qquad \cdot$$
$$F_n = \alpha_n x_1 + \beta_n x_2 + \ldots + \gamma_n x_m. \tag{3}$$

Then by manipulating these loadings to obtain equations for each factor, and substituting the different values of x variables into these equations, a set of factor 'scores', can be obtained which can be used to estimate the effect of each factor on price, as in equation (1).

9. For a review of various concepts of attraction, accessibility and potential see Vickerman (1974).

Chapter 4

1. It will be recalled from the discussion in Chapter One that the measurement of units of housing presents considerable problems. In most demand studies the practice of using an expenditure measure to express

quantity, on the assumption that the price per unit of housing is constant across the sample, is generally adopted.

2. For a more detailed explanation of demand equation estimation procedures and problems, with particular reference to housing, see Needleman (1965) ch. 3.

3. That the price elasticity of demand is equal to d_2 can be shown as follows:

If $h = d_0 y^{d_1} p^{d_2} i^{d_3}$

then $\dfrac{\partial h}{\partial p} = d_0 y^{d_1} d_2 p^{d_2 - 1} i^{d_3}$

and $\dfrac{p}{h} = \dfrac{p}{d_0 y^{d_1} p^{d_2} i^{d_3}}$,

so $\dfrac{\partial h}{\partial p} \cdot \dfrac{p}{h} = \dfrac{d_0 y^{d_1} d_2 p^{d_2} i^{d_3}}{d_0 y^{d_1} p^{d_2} i^{d_3}}$

$= d_2.$

Similar methods can be used to show that the income elasticity of demand is equal to d_1 and the interest rate elasticity equal to d_3.

4. Schwabe's 'law of rent' was named after Hermann Schwabe, Director of the Berlin Statistical Bureau, who proposed the relationship in 1867. Cited in Stigler (1954).

5. Cited in Reid (1962) pp. 1–2.

6. Friedman also divides consumer expenditure into permanent and transitory components although the distinction is not crucial for our exposition.

7. Winger (1963) concentrates upon the process whereby households upgrade their housing demand through movement by developing a model which attempts to predict those households who are in 'disequilibrium' and thus likely to move house.

8. See DeLeeuw (1971) for an explanation of why this is so.

9. Malinvaud (1970 pp. 281–5) explains how information is lost when data are grouped, so there is a tendency for estimates based on grouped data to be less efficient.

10. Byatt *et al.* (1973) p. 69.

11. For a guide to this literature see Whitehead (1974).

12. By substituting equation (4.7) on page 50 into equation (4.8) on the same page we obtain:

$$\Delta h = db_0 + db_1 p + db_2 y + db_3 i - dh \tag{A}$$

Now we wish to find

$$e_{h^*y} = \frac{\partial h^*}{\partial y} \cdot \frac{y}{h^*}$$

From equation (4.7) we know that

$$\frac{\partial h^*}{\partial y} = b_2,$$

so

$$\frac{\partial h^*}{\partial y} \cdot \frac{y}{h^*} = b_2 \frac{y}{h^*}.$$

Then multiplying the numerator and denominator by d, we obtain $\dfrac{db_2 y}{dh^*}$, which is evaluated as follows. First the term $db_2 y$ can be obtained from equation (A) above as db_2 will be approximated by the parameter estimate associated with y, whereas y itself can be evaluated at the sample mean point in the usual way. Second, dh^* can be obtained by multiplying both sides of equation (4.7) by d, as follows:

$$dh^* = db_0 + db_1 p + db_2 y + db_3 i \qquad (B)$$

The right-hand side of equation (B) is of course the same as the right-hand side of equation (A), but with the final term omitted. It can therefore be evaluated by taking the parameter estimates of equation (A) and the sample means of p, y and i.

13. Movement by existing households does not, of course, result in additional net demand because they also vacate dwellings as they move; it does, however, lead to changes in the demand for housing within particular tenure groups and also to the demand for new housing. Moreover it may also represent an increase in the demand for housing services, or attributes, as households use movement as a means of upgrading their accommodation.

14. Internal consistency requires, of course, that in each category the headship rate multiplied by the average family size = the total population.

15. Needleman (1965) p. 36.

Chapter 5

1. Bowley (1966) p. 439.

2. In addition to new housebuilding, the industry has substantial sectors devoted to industrial and commercial construction, as well as maintenance and repair business. Although many firms tend to specialise in a particular

type of work, there is a certain amount of movement between the sectors in response to fluctuations in demand. The following table indicates the relative importance of the different sectors in the period 1971–5.

Value of Output, £ million (1970 prices)

| | New work | | Repair and maintenance | | Total |
	Housing	Other	Housing	Other	
1971	1 629 (26 %)	2 857 (46 %)	765 (13 %)	931 (15 %)	6 182 (100 %)
72	1 915 (27)	3 118 (45)	940 (14)	1 047 (15)	7 020 (100)
73	2 541 (28)	3 921 (44)	1 277 (14)	1 256 (14)	8 995 (100)
74	2 595 (25)	4 598 (45)	1 503 (15)	1 494 (15)	10 190 (100)
75	3 031 (26)	5 146 (44)	1 659 (14)	1 774 (16)	11 610 (100)

Source: *Housing and Construction statistics.*

3. See Harrison (1977) for a discussion of the economic rationale for land-and-use planning.

4. For a discussion of the contemporary role of design professionals in the development process, see National Economic Development Office (1976 *a*).

5. The relative merits of different forms of tendering have attracted a good deal of attention; for a discussion of the issues involved, see Hillebrandt (1974) ch. 7.

6. See Needleman (1965) pp. 80–3.

7. In her analysis Hillebrandt distinguishes between changes in output that result from changes in the *size* of the contracts that a firm receives and those which result from changes in the *number* of contracts. Both affect the quantity of work per period of time but they may have different effects upon costs.

8. Hillebrandt defines a small firm as one employing fewer than twenty-five persons.

9. The existence of a large number of small firms specialising in maintenance and repair work may have direct implications for government policy choices. For example, Needleman (1965) argues that the existence of numerous small firms geared to repair work is one reason for preferring a policy of housing improvement to one of redevelopment. (See Chapter Seven).

10. Hillebrandt calculates that between 1959 and 1969 work in the small-firm sector grew by only 25 per cent compared with a 50 per cent growth rate for large firms. Moreover, since then their share of output has fallen even further: in 1969 they accounted for 23 per cent of the industry's net output whereas the Census data in Table 5.2 show that by 1974 this had dropped to 21 per cent.

11. From *Housing and Construction Statistics.*

12. Balchin and Kieve (1977) p. 249.

13. See Clark (1958).

14. Stone (1970) p. 121.

15. Needleman (1965) p. 91.

Chapter 6

1. See, for example, Lipsey (1975) pp. 117–19.
2. For a collection of such papers, see Hayek *et al.* (1972).
3. For example, see Cullingworth (1965), especially the introduction and chs 3 and 5.
4. This gap is far less pronounced in the American literature where there have been a number of econometric studies dealing with the effects of rent control. For example, see De Salvo (1970) and Olsen (1972).
5. The capital value of a property with a sitting tenant paying a controlled rent will be below its value with vacant possession. In many cases, the landlord's expectations about the time a tenancy will end, and the discount rate he employs, will combine to induce him to retain the property until he obtains vacant possession and can realise its higher capital value.
6. There are a number of books which provide more detailed accounts of rent-controlling legislation. For example, see Greve (1965) ch. 1. An excellent account of the evolution of rent control – and other housing policies – is also provided in Cullingworth (1966).
7. See Nevitt (1966) pp. 114–15.
8. See Phelps Brown and Wiseman (1964) p. 219.
9. Greve (1965) p. 16.
10. Donnison *et al.* (1961) ch. 2.
11. See Donnison *et al.* (1964) ch. 4 and Milner Holland (1965) pp. 325–7.
12. See Cullingworth (1963) p. 94.
13. Cullingworth found that many landlords were elderly retired persons who had invested their savings in one or two properties. The responses of these people to changes in economic circumstances can be expected to be very different from those of corporate landlords.
14. Data from *Housing and Construction Statistics*.
15. Greve (1965) p. 10.
16. See Donnison (1967*b*) p. 186.
17. Data from *Housing and Construction Statistics*.
18. Quoted in Cullingworth (1966) p. 18.
19. Milner Holland (1965) p. 362.
20. See Cullingworth (1965) p. 35.
21. See Woolf (1964) p. 35.
22. Reports quoted in Cullingworth (1966).
23. Donnison *et al.* (1961) p. 60.
24. Nevitt (1966) p. 47.
25. De Salvo (1970) p. 227.
26. Milner Holland (1965) p. 148.
27. Francis (1971) p. 137.
28. Francis (1971) p. 82.
29. Stafford (1973) p. 122.
30. See ch. 7 of the report.
31. This analysis is based on Robinson (1973); many of the same arguments are now more widely available in Cooper and Stafford (1975).
32. Francis (1971) p. 60.

33. For a discussion of procedures used to determine fair rents in practice see Macey (1972).

Chapter 7

1. The terms *renewal, rebuilding, redevelopment*, etc., are often used in an interchangeable fashion. In our discussions the term *renewal* will be used in a generic sense to refer to all forms of policy designed to replace slums and upgrade housing quality. Within this category *rebuilding* and *redevelopment* will be used to refer to schemes that involve the demolition of existing housing and its replacement by new dwellings, whereas *improvement, renovation* or *rehabilitation* will be used to refer to the upgrading of existing dwellings.

2. Ratcliff (1949) pp. 402–3.

3. The first explanation is sometimes taken to imply that slums result solely from the fall in demand from middle-income groups, but this view is inconsistent with evidence on the high profitability of slums. (See, for example, Sporn (1960).) A more convincing explanation is that falling demand on the part of high-income groups combined with a growth in demand *for low-quality housing* from low-income groups results in the creation of such areas.

4. A unit of housing service takes account of both the qualitative and quantitative aspects of housing produced by its various attributes. See Chapter One.

5. To simplify the exposition we have presented this example in terms of two alternatives: to invest in housing repairs or not to invest. Obviously, if a landlord does not invest, he incurs a *zero* cost and so any return received via external benefits will represent an infinite rate of return. Davis and Whinston avoid this problem by assuming that the landlord has an investment portfolio in which housing investment is but one component. Then, by assuming that the size and the rate of return on the non-housing part of the portfolio remains constant, fluctuations in housing returns will affect the average rate of return on the entire portfolio. These are the entries they include in their payoff matrix.

6. In some cases these will be straightforward technological external costs: for example, if a slum dweller contacts typhoid and transmits it to a non-slum dweller. In other cases, private costs will become pecuniary external costs if welfare services are financed publicly. For instance, the health care costs of a non-contagious disease will be transferred from the individual to society if there is a National Health Service.

7. See Spencer (1970) for data on take-up rates.

8. For example, see Cullingworth (1973) and Jacobs (1962).

9. For a selection of this literature see the readings edited by Wilson (1966). A British case study describing the complex issues involved in a renewal strategy is provided by Dennis (1970, 1972).

10. $\frac{r}{i}[1-(1+i)^{-\lambda}]$ is the present value of the excess annual running costs of a renovated property summed over its life of λ years and discounted

at *i*. This term is obtained from the conventional present value formula as follows:

$$PV = r \left[\frac{1}{1+i} + \frac{1}{(1+i)^2} + \frac{1}{(1+i)^3} + \ldots + \frac{1}{(1+i)^\lambda} \right]. \quad (1)$$

By multiplying both sides by $(1+i)$ we obtain:

$$(1+i)PV = r(1+i)\left[\frac{1}{1+i} + \frac{1}{(1+i)^2} + \ldots + \frac{1}{(1+i)^\lambda} \right]$$

$$= r\left[1 + \frac{1}{1+i} + \frac{1}{(1+i)^2} \cdots \frac{1}{(1+i)^{\lambda-1}} \right]. \quad (2)$$

Then, by subtracting (1) from (2), we obtain:

$$(1+i)PV - PV = r\left[1 - \frac{1}{(1+i)^\lambda} \right]$$

$$\text{or} \quad PV = \frac{r}{i}\left[1 - \frac{1}{(1+i)^\lambda} \right]. \quad (3)$$

11. There are numerous books which explain the theory and application of cost-benefit analysis. See, for example, Layard (1974), Mishan (1971*a*) and Dasgupta and Pearce (1972).

12. Rothenberg (1967) p. 118.

13. Even this measure would, of course, require a series of stringent assumptions to be met before it could be considered to produce a satisfactory measure of overall benefit. Notably, it would require the marginal utility of income to be constant across tenants before aggregation could take place.

14. See Commission on the Third London Airport (1970) *Papers and Proceedings*, vol. VII. (London: HMSO).

15. See County Borough of Brighton (1972) *Central Whitehawk: re-development v. modernisation*.

16. For an alternative view of the political significance of cost-benefit analysis see Self (1975).

Chapter 8

1. For a fuller account of the historical origins of LA housing, see Cullingworth (1966) ch. 1

2. The Community Development Project (CDP) Report (1976) describes the effect of changes in the political climate on council housing.

3. See Garfinkel (1973) for elaboration of this point.

4. On a more general level there is always the rejoinder which points out that the analysis of Figure 8.2 is a partial one which ignores the possible

distortionary effects of an income supplement that may arise in other markets. For example, income subsidies may well distort an individual's work–leisure choice and thereby lead to a loss of efficiency in the labour market in a way that a housing price subsidy would not.

5. Le Grand (1975) has pointed out that, in principle, the government can, by using a policy of price subsidisation, ensure the consumption of a predetermined quantity of a commodity by manipulating prices so that the individual chooses the required quantity freely. In practice, however, this procedure would involve considerable problems, especially if heterogeneous preferences meant that prices had to be household-specific.

6. This account should not be taken to imply that LAs actually use a formula such as that shown in equation (8.1) to determine rent levels; but that their practices approximate the procedures described here.

7. See Parker (1967).

8. See U. K. Department of the Environment (1977), *Housing Policy: A Consultative Document*, table 10, p. 147 and table 18, p. 153.

9. Op. cit. p. 83.

10. There are many writers who discuss the theory and practice of marginal cost pricing. See, for example, Phelps Brown and Wiseman (1964) ch. vi and Gwilliam and Mackie (1975) ch. 6.

11. Harrison (1977) ch. 8 develops this point.

12. Other more conventional objections to marginal cost pricing may also be advanced. Notably, if the policy is not employed in other sectors of the housing market there is no guarantee that its adoption in the LA sector will produce an efficient outcome.

13. See CDP Report (1976) p. 27.

Chapter 9

1. See the *Guardian* newspaper letters column and editorials between 30 July and 6 August 1977 for a particularly lively and amusing debate on this subject.

2. UK Department of the Environment (1977), *Housing Policy: a Consultative Document*, p. 49.

3. Tax relief on interest payments will, of course, vary with the interest rate and so if increases in house price reflect general price movements – including the price of credit – the amount of tax relief will also vary.

4. This point can be illustrated through the use of indifference-curve analysis. A change in the relative prices of housing and non-housing goods, together with an outward shift in the budget constraint resulting from the real balance effect will present the scope for a welfare gain. Moreover, the position of the existing owner will clearly be preferable to that of the prospective first-time buyer who faces an increase in relative prices but receives no increase in the value of his real balances.

5. Imputed income is used in the case of company cars to determine liability to personal income taxation but not in cases where the individual owns his car.

6. Many writers when confronted with this question refer to Muth (1960),

who on the basis of US data argues that in the long run the supply of housing is highly elastic. However, as we saw in Chapter Four, Muth's results suggest that only 30 per cent of any discrepancy between a desired and actual stock will be eliminated each year. This suggests considerable inelasticity in the short run; for example, it suggests that it will take six years before 90 per cent of any shortfall will be met. Our analysis of the housing supply industry in Chapter Five also leads us to expect price inelasticity.

7. See U.K. Department of the Environment (1977) *Housing Policy: Technical Volume*, part ii, ch. 5.

8. Option mortgages are loans provided to the borrower at below market interest rates. They offer assistance to those low-income borrowers whose earnings are insufficient to benefit from exemption from income tax.

9. Property bought with building society mortgages will tend to under-represent more expensive dwellings and also, of course, many owners will be liable to higher than standard rates of taxation. (The majority of housing – which is not traded – will tend to have higher floor prices than comparable traded property; this will lead to an underestimate of average imputed income but will not necessarily distort comparisons between owner-occupier and LA tenant households because the same underestimate is incorporated in Rosenthal's calculations as they are also based on the prices of traded property.)

10. Rent allowances represent less than 2 per cent of total housing assistance; see Boyd (1977).

11. Again, see Boyd (1977).

Bibliography

Adamson, Sally (1974), 'The Politics of Improvement Grants', *Town Planning Review*, vol. 45, pp. 375–86.

Alonso, W. (1964), *Location and Land Use: Towards a General Theory of Land Rent* (Cambridge, Mass.: Harvard University Press).

Anderson, Martin (1964), *The Federal Bulldozer: A Critical Analysis of Urban Renewal* (Cambridge, Mass.: M.I.T. Press).

Balchin, Paul N., and Kieve, Jeffrey L. (1977), *Urban Land Economics* (London: Macmillan).

Ball, Michael J. (1973), 'Recent Empirical Work on the Determinants of Relative House Prices', *Urban Studies*, vol. 10, pp. 213–33.

— (1974), 'The Determinants of Relative House Prices: a Reply', *Urban Studies*, vol. 11, pp. 231–3.

— and Kirwan, Richard (1975), *The Economics of an Urban Housing Market* (London: Centre for Environmental Studies).

— (1977), 'Accessibility and Supply Constraints in the Urban Housing Market', *Urban Studies*, vol. 14, pp. 11–32.

Black, J. (1974), 'A New System of Mortgages', *Lloyds Bank Review*, January.

Blank, D. M., and Winnick, L. (1953), 'The Structure of the Housing Market', *Quarterly Journal of Economics*, vol. 67, pp. 11–32.

Bowley, Marian (1945), *Housing and the State, 1919–1944* (London: Allen & Unwin).

— (1966), *The British Building Industry* (Cambridge University Press).

Boyd, Chris (1977), 'A Fair Share', *Roof*, September.

Byatt, I. C. R., Holmans, A. E., and Laidler, D. E. W. (1973), 'Income and the Demand for Housing: some evidence for Great Britain', in *Essays in Modern Economics*, ed. M. Parkin and A. R. Nobay (London: Longmans).

Carliner, Geoffrey (1973), 'Income Elasticity of Housing Demand', *Review of Economics and Statistics*, vol. 55, pp. 528–32.

Christ, Carl F. (1966), *Econometric Models and Methods* (New York: Wiley & Sons).

Clark, Colin (1958), 'The Economics of High Building', *Town and Country Planning*, vol. 26, pp. 73–5.

— (1966), 'Urban Land Use Here and Abroad', *Journal of the Town Planning Institute*, vol. 52, pp. 359–64.

— and Jones, G. T. (1971), *The Demand for Housing*, University Working Paper no. 11 (London: Centre for Environmental Studies).

Cleary, E. J. (1965), *The Building Society Movement* (London: Elek).

Colclough, J. R. (1965), *The Construction Industry of Great Britain* (London: Butterworths).

Commission on the Third London Airport (1970), *Papers and Proceedings*, vol. VII (London: H.M.S.O.).

Community Development Project (1976), *Whatever Happened to Council Housing?* (London: C.D.P. Information and Intelligence Unit).

Cooper, M. H., and Stafford, D. C. (1975), 'A Note on the Economic Implications of Fair Rents', *Social and Economic Administration*, vol. 9, pp. 26–9.

County Borough of Brighton (1972), *Central Whitehawk: Redevelopment v. Modernisation* (Brighton: Borough Treasurer's Department).

Crouch, Colin, and Wolf, Martin (1972), 'Inequality in Housing', in *Labour and Inequality*, ed. Peter Townsend and Nicholas Bosanquet (London: Fabian Society).

Cullingworth, J. B. (1960), *Housing Needs and Planning Policy* (London: Routledge & Kegan Paul).

— (1963), *Housing in Transition* (London: Heinemann).

— (1965), *English Housing Trends*, Occasional Papers in Social Administration, no. 13 (London: Bell & Sons).

— (1966), *Housing and Local Government* (London: Allen & Unwin).

— (1973), *Problems of Urban Society*, vol. II: *The Social Context of Planning* (London: Allen & Unwin).

Dasgupta, A. K., and Pearce, D. W. (1972), *Cost–Benefit Analysis: Theory and Practice* (London: Macmillan).

Davidson, B. R. (1975), 'The Effects of Land Speculation on the Supply of Housing in England and Wales', *Urban Studies*, vol. 12, pp. 91–9.

Davies, Graham (1974), 'An Econometric Analysis of Residential Amenity', *Urban Studies*, vol. 11, pp. 217–25.

Davis, Otto, and Whinston, Andrew (1961), 'Economics of Urban Renewal', *Law and Contemporary Problems*, vol. 26, pp. 106–17.

DeLeeuw, Frank (1971), 'The Demand for Housing: a Review of Cross-Section Evidence', *Review of Economics and Statistics*, vol. 53, pp. 1–10.

De Salvo, J. S. (1970), 'Reforming Rent Control in New York City', *Papers and Proceedings of the Regional Science Association*, no. 27, pp. 195–227.

Dennis, Norman (1970), *People and Planning* (London: Faber & Faber).

— (1972), *Public Participation and Planner's Blight* (London: Faber & Faber).

Doling, J. F. (1973), 'A Two-Stage Model of Tenure Choice in the Housing Market', *Urban Studies*, vol. 10, pp. 199–21.

Donnison, D. V. (1967a), 'The Political Economy of Housing', in *The Economic Problems of Housing*, ed. A. A. Nevitt (London: Macmillan).

— (1967b), *The Government of Housing* (Harmondsworth: Penguin Books).

—, Cockburn, C., and Corbett, T. (1961), *Housing Since the Rent Act*, Occasional Papers on Social Administration, no. 3 (Welwyn: Codicote Press).

—, —, Cullingworth, J. B., and Nevitt, A. A. (1964), *Essays on Housing*, Occasional Papers on Social Administration, no. 9 (Welwyn: Codicote Press).

Edel, Matthew (1972), 'Filtering in a Private Housing Market', in *Readings in Urban Economics*, ed. Matthew Edel and Jerome Rothenberg (New York: Macmillan).

Evans, A. W. (1973), *The Economics of Residential Location* (London: Macmillan).

Eversley, David (1975), 'Landlords' Slow Goodbye', *New Society*, 16 January.
Firestone, O. J. (1951), *Residential Real Estate in Canada* (University of Toronto Press).
Fisher, E. M., and Winnick, L. (1951), 'Reformulation of the Filtering Concept', *Journal of Social Issues*, vol. 7, pp. 47–58.
Francis, H. E., Chairman (1971), *Report of the Committee on the Rent Acts*, Cmnd 4609 (London: H.M.S.O.).
Frankena, Mark (1975), 'Alternative Models of Rent Control', *Urban Studies*, vol. 12, pp. 303–8.
Friedman, M. (1957), *A Theory of the Consumption Function*, National Bureau of Economic Research (Princeton, N.J.: Princeton University Press).
— and Stigler, G. (1972), 'Roofs or Ceilings?', in *Verdict on Rent Control*, ed. F. A. Hayek *et al.* (London: Institute of Economic Affairs).
Fuerst, J. S. (ed.) (1974), *Public Housing in Europe and America* (London: Croom Helm).
Garfinkel, Irwin (1973), 'Is In-Kind Redistribution Efficient?', *Quarterly Journal of Economics*, vol. 87, pp. 320–30.
Gelfand, Jack E. (1966), 'The Credit Elasticity of Lower-Middle-Income Housing Demand', *Land Economics*, vol. 42, pp. 464–72.
Ghosh, D. (1974), *The Economics of Building Societies* (Farnborough, Hants: Saxon House).
Goodall, Brian (1972), *The Economics of Urban Areas* (Oxford: Pergamon Press).
Gray, P. G., and Parr, E. (1960), *Rent Act 1957; Report of Inquiry* (London: H.M.S.O.).
— and Russell, R. (1962), *The Housing Situation in 1960*, The Social Survey (London: Central Office of Information).
Grebler, L., Blank, D., and Winnick, L. (1956), *Capital Formation in Residential Real Estate* (Princeton, N. J.: Princeton University Press).
Greve, John (1965), *Private Landlords in England*, Occasional Papers on Social Administration, no. 16 (London: Bell & Sons).
Grigsby, William G. (1963), *Housing Markets and Public Policy* (Philadelphia: University of Pennsylvania Press).
Guttentag, J. M. (1961), 'The Short Cycle in Residential Construction, 1946–59', *American Economic Review*, vol. 51, pp. 275–98.
Gwilliam, K. M., and Mackie, P. J. (1975), *Economics and Transport Policy* (London: Allen & Unwin).
Hadjimatheou, George (1976), *Housing and Mortgage Markets* (Farnborough, Hants: Saxon House).
Harloe, M., Issacharoff, R., and Minns, R. (1974), *The Organisation of Housing* (London: Heinemann).
Harrington, R. L. (1972), 'Housing – Supply and Demand', *National Westminster Bank Quarterly Review*, May.
Harrison, A. J. (1977), *Economics and Land Use Planning* (London: Croom Helm).
Hayek, F. A., *et al.* (1972), *Verdict on Rent Control* (London: Institute of Economic Affairs).
Heilbrun, James (1974), *Urban Economics and Public Policy* (New York: St Martin's Press).

Hillebrandt, Patricia M. (1971), *Small Firms in the Construction Industry*, Committee of Inquiry on Small Firms, Research Report no. 10 (London: H.M.S.O.).

— (1974), *Economic Theory and the Construction Industry* (London: Macmillan).

Holmans, A. E. (1970), 'A Forecast of Effective Demand for Housing in Great Britain in the 1970's', *Social Trends*, no. 1 (London: H.M.S.O.).

Holtermann, Sally (1975), 'Areas of Urban Deprivation in Great Britain: An Analysis of 1971 Census Data', *Social Trends* (London: H.M.S.O.)

Jacobs, Jane (1962), *The Death and Life of Great American Cities* (London: Cape).

Jones, Colin (1976), 'Household Movement, Filtering and Home Ownership', Paper delivered to the S.S.R.C. Urban and Regional Studies Seminar, Polytechnic of Central London, December.

Kain, John F., and Quigley, John M. (1970), 'Measuring the Value of Housing Quality', *Journal of the American Statistical Association*, vol. 65, pp. 532–48

Kemp, Frances M. (1974), 'The Comparative Economics of Rehabilitation and Redevelopment with Reference to an Area of Brighton', B.A. dissertation, University of Sussex.

Kirwan, R. M., and Martin, D. B. (1972), *The Economics of Urban Residential Renewal and Improvement*, Working Paper no. 77 (London: Centre for Environmental Studies).

Lancaster, Kelvin J. (1966), 'A New Approach to Consumer Theory', *Journal of Political Economy*, vol. 74, pp. 132–57.

Layard, Richard (ed.) (1974), *Cost–Benefit Analysis* (Harmondsworth, Middlesex: Penguin Books).

Le Grand, Julian (1975) 'Public Price Discrimination and Aid to Low Income Groups', *Economica*, vol. 42, pp. 32–45.

Lee, Tong Hun (1963), 'Demand for Housing: A Cross-Section Analysis', *Review of Economics and Statistics*, vol. 45, pp. 190–6.

— (1968), 'Housing and Permanent Income: Tests based on a Three-Year Re-Interview Survey', *Review of Economics and Statistics*, vol. 50, pp. 480–90.

Lichfield, N., Kettle, P., and Whitbread, M. (1975), *Evaluation in the Planning Process* (Oxford: Pergamon Press).

Lipsey, Richard G. (1975), *An Introduction to Positive Economics*, 4th ed. (London: Weidenfeld & Nicolson).

Lowry, Ira S. (1960), 'Filtering and Housing Standards: a Conceptual Analysis', *Land Economics*, vol. 36, pp. 362–70.

Macey, G. (1972), 'How to Assess a Fair Rent', *New Society*, July.

McKie, Robert (1971), *Housing and the Whitehall Bulldozer*, Hobart Paper no. 52 (London: Institute of Economic Affairs).

Maisel, S. J. (1971), 'The Demand for Housing: a Comment', *Review of Economics and Statistics*, vol. 53, pp. 410–13.

— and Winnick, L. (1960), 'Family Housing Expenditures: Elusive Laws and Intrusive Variances', in W. L. C. Wheaten, G. Milgram and M. E. Meyerson, *Urban Housing* (Free Press: New York).

Malinvaud, E. (1970), *Statistical Methods in Econometrics* (Amsterdam: North-Holland).

Medhurst, Franklin, and Parry Lewis, J. (1969), *Urban Decay: an Analysis and a Policy* (London: Macmillan).

Merrett, A. J., and Sykes, Allen (1965), *Housing Finance and Development* (London: Longmans).

Milner Holland, Chairman (1965). *Report of the Committee on Housing in Greater London*, Cmnd 2605 (London:H.M.S.O.).

Mishan, E. J. (1971*a*), *Cost-Benefit Analysis* (London: Allen & Unwin).

— (1971*b*), 'Evaluation of Life and Limb: a Theoretical Approach', *Journal of Political Economy*, vol. 79, pp. 687–705.

Moorhouse, J. C. (1972), 'Optimal Housing Maintenance under Rent Control', *Southern Economic Journal*, vol. 39, pp. 93–106.

Murie, Alan (1977), 'No Jackpot from Council House Sales', *Roof*, May.

Muth, R. F. (1960), 'The Demand for Non-Farm Housing', in *The Demand for Durable Goods*, ed. A. C. Harberger (University of Chicago Press).

— (1969), *Cities and Housing* (University of Chicago Press).

National Economic Development Office (1975), *The Public Client and the Construction Industries*, Building and Civil Engineering E.D.C. (London: H.M.S.O.).

— (1976*a*), *The Professions in the Construction Industries*, Building and Civil Engineering E.D.C. (London: H.M.S.O.).

— (1976*b*), *Construction in the Early 1980s*, Building and Civil Engineering E.D.C. (London: H.M.S.O.).

Needleman, L. (1961), 'A Long-Term View of Housing', *National Institute Economic Review*, no. 18, November.

— (1965), *The Economics of Housing* (London: Staples Press).

— (1968), 'Rebuilding or Renovation? A Reply', *Urban Studies*, vol. 5, pp. 86–90.

— (1969), 'The Comparative Economics of Improvement and New Building', *Urban Studies*, vol. 6, pp. 196–209.

Neuburger, H. L. I., and Nichol, B. M. (1976), *The Recent Course of Land and Property Prices and the Factors Underlying It*, Research Report 4 (London: Department of the Environment).

Nevitt, A. A. (1966), *Housing, Taxation and Subsidies* (London: Nelson).

— (ed.) (1967), *The Economic Problems of Housing* (London: Macmillan).

O'Herlihy, St J. C., and Spencer, J. E. (1972), 'Building Societies' Behaviour, 1955–70', *National Institute Economic Review*, no. 61, August.

Olsen, Edgar O. (1969), 'A Competitive Theory of the Housing Market', *American Economic Review*, vol. 59, pp. 612–22.

— (1972), 'An Econometric Analysis of Rent Control', *Journal of Political Economy*, vol. 80, pp. 1081–100.

Parker, R. A. (1967), *The Rents of Council Houses*, Occasional Papers on Social Administration, no. 22 (London: Bell & Sons).

Partridge, T. J. (1971), *The Filtering Process and Public Housing Policy*, Paper delivered to Urban Economics Conference sponsored by Centre for Environmental Studies, University of Keele.

Pennance, F. G., and West, W. (1969), *Housing Market Analysis and Policy*, Hobart Paper no. 48 (London: Institute of Economic Affairs).

Phelps Brown, E. H., and Wiseman, J. (1964), *A Course in Applied Economics* (London: Pitman).

Ratcliff, Richard U. (1949), *Urban Land Economics* (New York: McGraw-Hill).

Reid, Margaret G. (1962), *Housing and Income* (University of Chicago Press).

Riley, Kathleen M. (1973), 'An Estimate of the Age Distribution of the Dwelling Stock in Great Britain', *Urban Studies*, vol. 10, pp. 373–9.

Robinson, R. V. F. (1973), 'A Note on the Economics of Fair Rents', Paper delivered to the Regional Science Association Seminar, University of Sussex.

Rosenthal, L. (1975), 'The Nature of Council House Subsidies', unpublished Ph.D. thesis, University of Essex.

— (1977), 'The Regional and Income Distribution of the Council House Subsidy in the United Kingdom', *The Manchester School*, vol. 45, pp. 127–40.

Rothenberg, Jerome (1967), *Economic Evaluation of Urban Renewal* (Washington, D.C.: Brookings Institution).

Seeley, Ivor H. (1974), *Building Economics* (London: Macmillan).

Self, Peter (1975), *Econocrats and the Policy Process* (London: Macmillan).

Shea, Charles (1971), 'House Purchase – The Case for a Junior Mortgage Market', *National Westminster Bank Quarterly Review*, February.

Sigsworth, E. M., and Wilkinson, R. K. (1967), 'Rebuilding or Renovation?' *Urban Studies*, vol. 4, pp. 109–21.

— (1970), 'Rebuilding or Renovation? A Rejoinder', *Urban Studies*, vol. 7, pp. 92–4.

Smith, David L. (1974), *Amenity and Urban Planning* (London: Crosby Lockwood & Staples).

Smith, Wallace F. (1970), *Housing: The Social and Economic Elements* (Berkeley: University of California Press).

— (1972), A Theory of Filtering', in *Readings in Urban Economics*, ed. Matthew Edel and Jerome Rothenberg (New York: Macmillan).

Smolensky, E., Becker, S., and Molotch, H. (1968), 'The Prisoner's Dilemma and Ghetto Expansion', *Land Economics*, vol. 44, pp. 419–30.

Spencer, K. M. (1970), 'Older Areas and Housing Improvement Policies', *Town Planning Review*, vol. 41, pp. 250–62.

Sporn, Arthur D. (1960), 'Empirical Studies in the Economics of Slum Ownership', *Land Economics*, vol. 36, pp. 333–40.

Stafford, D. C. (1973), 'A Survey of Recent Developments in Housing Legislation, Policy and Administration', *Social and Economic Administration*, vol. 7. pp. 106—25.

Stigler, G. (1954), 'The Early History of Empirical Studies of Consumer Behaviour', *Journal of Political Economy*, vol. 62, pp. 95–113.

Stone, P. A. (1965), 'The Prices of Building Sites in Britain', in *Land Values*, ed. Peter Hall (London: Sweet & Maxwell).

— (1966), *Building Economy* (Oxford: Pergamon Press).

— (1970), *Urban Development in Britain: Standards, Costs and Resources, 1964—2004*, vol. 1 (Cambridge University Press).

Stonier, Alfred W., and Hague, Douglas C. (1972), *A Textbook of Economic*

Theory, 4th ed. (London: Longmans).

Turvey, R. (1957), *The Economics of Real Property* (London: Allen & Unwin).

U. K. Central Statistical Office (1968), 'House Condition Survey, England and Wales, 1967', *Economic Trends*, May.

U.K. Department of the Environment (1973), *House Condition Survey, England and Wales, 1971*, Housing Survey Reports no. 9 (London: H.M.S.O.).

— (1977), *Housing Policy: A Consultative Document*, Cmnd 6851 (London: H.M.S.O.).

U.K. Ministry of Housing and Local Government (1968), *Old Houses into New Homes*, Cmnd 3602 (London: H.M.S.O.).

— (1969), *Council Housing: Purposes, Procedures and Priorities* (London: H.M.S.O.).

Vickerman, R. W. (1974), 'Accessibility, Attraction and Potential: a Review of Some Concepts and Their Use in Determining Mobility', *Environment and Planning*, vol. 6, pp. 675–91.

Vipond, J., and Walker, J. B. (1972), 'The Determinants of Housing Expenditure and Owner Occupation', *Bulletin of the Oxford University Institute of Economics and Statistics*, vol. 34, pp. 169–87.

Wabe, J. S. (1971), 'A Study of House Prices as a Means of Establishing the Value of Journey Time, the Rate of Time Preference, and the Valuation of Some Aspects of Environment in the London Metropolitan Region', *Applied Economics*, vol. 3, pp. 247–55.

Whitehead, C. M. E. (1971), 'A Model of the U.K. Housing Market', *Bulletin of the Oxford University Institute of Economics and Statistics*, vol. 33, pp. 245–66.

Whitehead, C. M. E. (1974), *The U.K. Housing Market: An Econometric Model* (Farnborough, Hants: Saxon House).

— and Odling-Smee, J. C. (1975), 'Long-Run Equilibrium in Urban Housing – A Note', *Urban Studies*, vol. 12, pp. 315–18.

Wilkinson, R. K. (1971), 'The Determinants of Relative House Prices', Paper delivered to the Urban Economics Conference sponsored by the Centre for Environmental Studies, University of Keele.

— and Gulliver, S. (1971), 'The Economics of Housing: A Survey', *Social and Economic Administration*, vol. 5, pp. 83–99.

— (1973), 'House Prices and the Measurement of Externalities', *Economic Journal*, vol. 83, pp. 72–86.

— (1974), 'The Determinants of Relative House Prices: A Case of Academic Astigmatism?', *Urban Studies*, vol. 11, pp. 227–30.

Williams, Peter (1976), *The Role of Financial Institutions and Estate Agents in the Private Housing Market*, Working Paper no. 39 (Centre for Urban and Regional Studies, University of Birmingham).

Wilson, James Q. (ed.) (1966), *Urban Renewal: The Record and the Controversy* (Cambridge, Mass.: M.I.T. Press).

Winger, Alan R. (1963), 'An Approach to Measuring Potential Upgrading Demand in the Housing Market', *Review of Economics and Statistics*, vol. 45, pp. 239–44.

Winger, Alan R. (1968), 'Housing and Income', *Western Economic Journal*, vol. 6, pp. 226–32.

Wingo, Lowden (1961), *Transportation and Urban Land* (Washington, D.C.: Resources for the Future).

Woolf, Myra (1964), *The Housing Survey in England and Wales*, Government Social Survey (London: H.M.S.O.).

Wray, M. (1968), 'Building Society Mortgages and the Housing Market', *National Westminster Bank Quarterly Review*, February.

Author Index

Subject Index

7468